Behind the Scenes

The most comprehensive illustrated guide to professional makeup artistry

By
HELEN HALL McLEAN

Illustrations by
DJAEF MAHLER

Lithographed and bound in Canada by
Evergreen Press Limited,
Vancouver, British Columbia

CONTENTS

INTRODUCTION

Now after many years of research and extensive development in the field of makeup artistry, we bring you "Behind the Scenes", the first book written with the express purpose of unveiling the techniques and secrets of professional makeup artists. The techniques have been presented in a simplified method of application to enable you to learn quickly and easily — and still achieve professional results. This text is precise, to the point and easy to follow with explicit illustrations that enable you to relate to the instructions.

Many of the worlds most admired women owe their beauty to their makeup artist or their own acquired knowledge of makeup artistry. We believe every woman can be more beautiful but that few women know how to go about achieving their ultimate beauty potential. This book was written with the express purpose of making it possible for any woman to learn to become her own makeup artist.

The makeup techniques introduced in the following pages are timeless and will stay with you over the years as they are based on the natural facial structure. Once you have learned the basic principles of makeup artistry, you will be able to adapt easily to any makeup variation in order to keep abreast with the current fashion trends.

"Behind the Scenes" should be used, not just read and should be referred to as often as necessary until you have mastered the techniques.

PROFESSIONAL MAKEUP BRUSHES

If you can relate makeup artistry to an artist painting a picture, you will understand the importance of your brushes. An artist would not attempt to paint a picture without the correct brushes. The same applies to makeup application. Lesson number one — in learning to become your own makeup artist, a set of professional makeup brushes is essential in order to achieve professional results in your application.

A good makeup brush is made of natural hair and has been designed for a specific purpose based on the experience of professional makeup artists.

#00 Eyeliner brush
The smallest brush of all, designed with a fine point. Perfect for outlining the eyes, "highlighting" fine lines and creases, and applying brow makeup, to simulate the fine hairs.

#6 Shadow brush
A straight edge brush suitable for applying cream and powder shadows to the lid, highlighting the brow bone, and for shading the eyes when using cream shadow.

#8 Shading brush
Similar to the #6 brush but wider, used primarily for shading the nose.

#7 Fluff brush
This is a round-tipped brush used for shading the brow bone when using a powder shadow. Also ideal for blending eye shadows.

#4 Wedge brush
Shaped at an angle, this brush is used for brow makeup application, in addition to being used for detailed eye shadow application — under the bottom lashes — inner depth shading — blending eye liner to soften and smudge edges.

#5 Eye brow brush
This brush resembles a miniature tooth brush. It is used to brush the brows into place as well as for brushing and separating the lashes.

#3 Contour brush
A flat-tipped brush designed to shade the hollows of the cheekbone, jawbone, forehead and the outer areas of the face.

#2 Rouge brush
A round-tipped brush with correct splay necessary for correct powder rouge application.

#1 Powder brush
A round-tipped brush for applying powder to the broad area of the face.

#9 Lip brush
A flat-tipped brush for perfect application of lipstick and lip sheen.

Double end applicator
For applying concealer, cream shadow, and blending eye liner.

Foam sponge
Used to achieve a smooth, even application of foundation and for cream rouge or shading application.

CREATING A BALANCED BROW

The brows are neglected by women probably more than any other single area of the face.

All effort put forth to makeup the eyes will be in vain if the brows have not been properly shaped.

Improperly shaped brows draw attention away from the eyes and give the whole face an unbalanced appearance. The most common mistakes made in brow shaping are — too thin, short, spaced wide apart, too close and drooped or incorrectly arched.

The eyebrows should be considered a frame for the eyes. When selecting a frame for a picture you would not choose one that would overpower or detract, the idea would be to complement and enhance the picture. The same principle applies to the brows. The result of properly proportioned brows should balance the eyes and flatter the individual facial features.

These illustrated examples clearly indicate how improperly shaped brows can affect the overall appearance of the eyes.

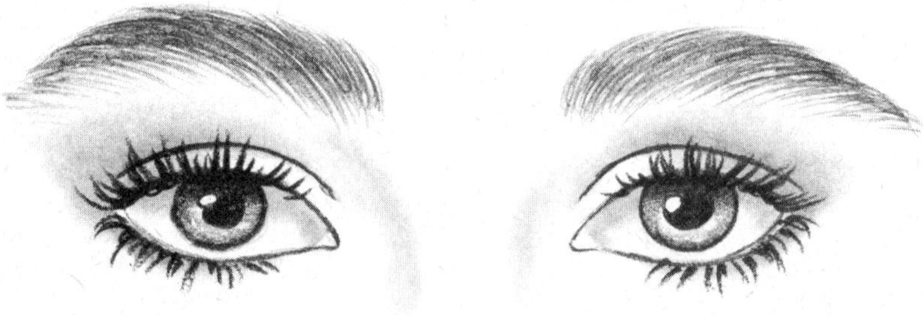

Thick brows with stray hairs growing down, close the space between the crease and the brows.

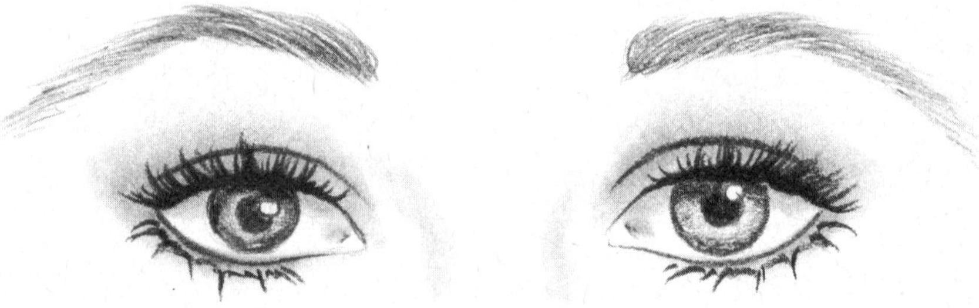

Stray hairs growing down in the outer area of the brow give the illusion of drooping eyes.

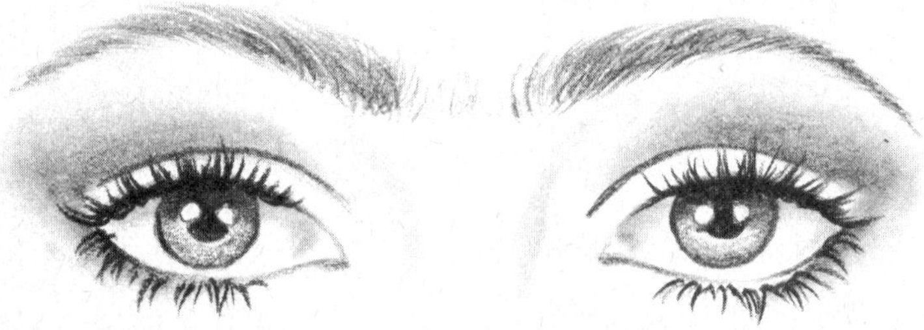

When the brows grow too far in from the inner corner they give the eyes the appearance of being too close together.

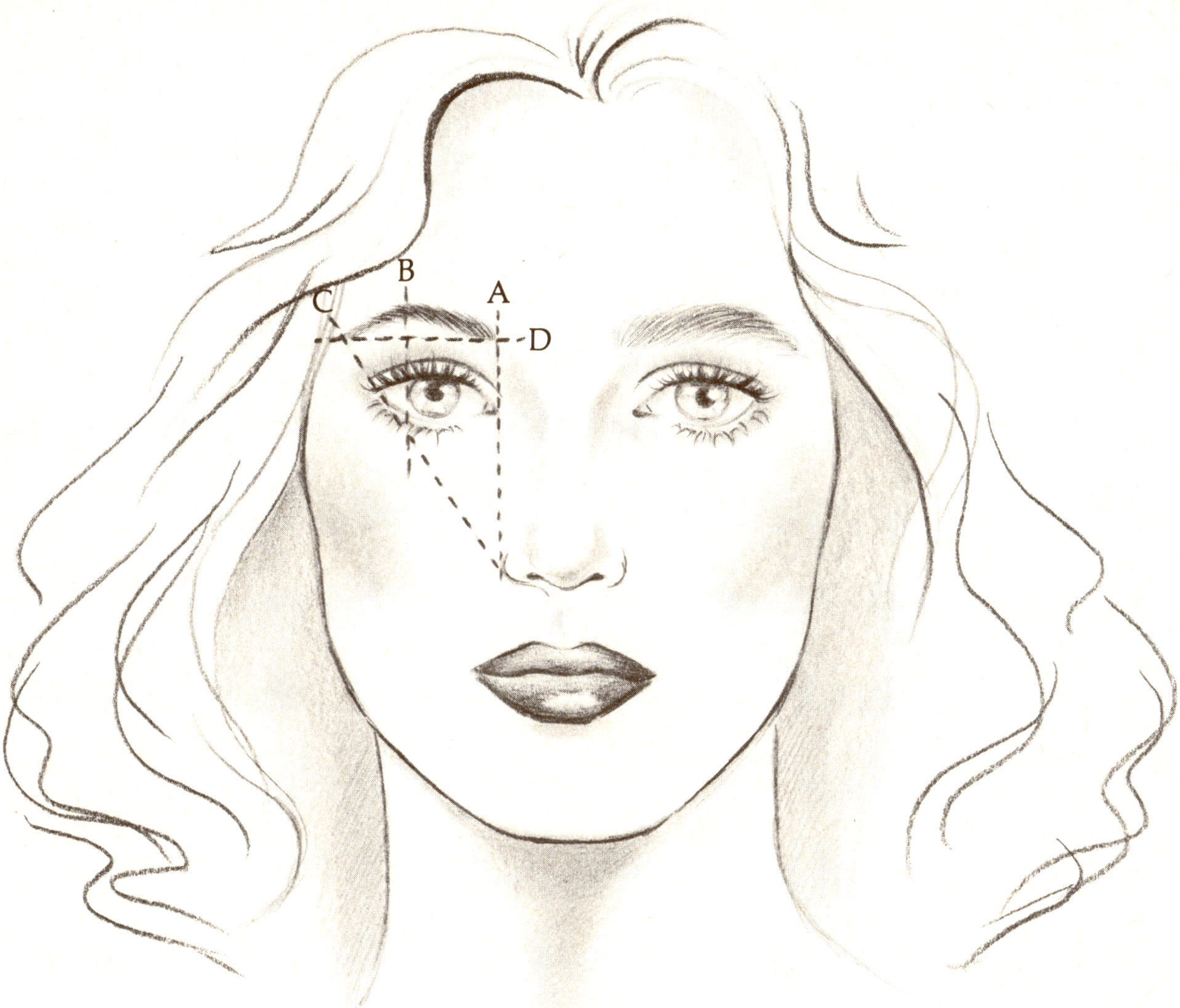

How to Create a Balanced Brow

To achieve properly proportioned brows follow these very simple guidelines.

A. The brow should begin directly over the inner corner of the eye. This can easily be determined by holding a pencil along the side of the nose and aligning it to the inner eye corner.

B. The arch should be approximately at the outer rim of the iris.

C. The brow should taper off at a position determined by holding a pencil to the side of the nose and the outer corner of the eye.

D. Where the brow begins and where it ends should be on the same level.

Corrective Shaping

Any corrective shaping or application of brow makeup must be very subtle. Do not detract from the appearance of a natural looking brow.

High forehead
The arch should be only slightly elevated. A definite high arch would only add to the appearance of a high forehead.

Low forehead
Keep the arch low. A higher arch closes the space giving the appearance of an even lower forehead.

Round face
Arch the brow slightly higher to create an illusion of length.

Long face
Very little arch is needed to create width.

Close-set eyes
Tweeze slightly at the inner corners to produce more space.

Wide-set eyes
Extend slightly inside the inner corner, thus giving the illusion of less space between the eyes.

General rules for tweezing

- Always tweeze the brows in the direction of the hair growth.
- Follow the natural curve of the brow bone.
- Tweeze from below, not above the brows. (There are rare exceptions to this rule).
- Grasp one hair at a time, pulling in very fast motions.
- Tweeze each row separately, from the inner to the outer corner.
- Take time to stop and analyse the effect of each row. Be careful not to get carried away and over tweeze.
- If your brows are thick and unruly, it is advisable to have a professional brow arch. Once you have a correctly balanced shape you will then find it easy to maintain by tweezing the stray hairs as necessary.
- Follow tweezing with an application of skin freshener, alcohol, or antiseptic followed by a moisturizer.

THE PRINCIPLE OF CONTOURING

Did you ever wonder how famous movie stars and models always appear to have beautiful high cheek bones and finely sculptured features?

Natural beauties are rare. It is through the techniques of makeup artistry that these results are achieved.

The techniques covered in the following pages will enable you to learn skills of highlighting and shading to minimize flaws and accentuate your best features.

First of all, let us define the word "Contouring".

The term, "Contouring" as it is used in makeup artistry is best explained as the combination of both *shading* and *highlighting* to change the "Contours" of the face.

It is important to add, however, that even though you can contour with light and dark in creating shape, the expression "Contouring" is more commonly used when referring to "Shading".

Shading

This is the application of a colour which is *darker* than the surrounding colours. Dark colours make an area appear receded (pushed back) or look smaller. They minimize and subdue features that are too prominent or unflattering. In addition, shading is used to dramatize and accentuate, e.g. under the cheekbone to optically deepen the hollow, to further augment the height and structure of the cheekbone, and also to create more depth and shape in the eye area.

Highlighting

The application of a colour which is *lighter* than the surrounding colours. Light colours bring an area forward, lift out of the shadows, and also enhance or emphasize the features.

Blending

Basically, all makeup artistry is creating illusions. To be successful, the art of "blending" must be perfected, and should be considered the most important technique for you to master, in developing as a makeup artist. Blending is graduating the intensity of a shade from its deepest to its lightest tone. The result of careful blending should make it impossible to see where a particular shade begins or ends. *Never* allow a hard line of demarcation to be observed. The colours must create the illusion of *real* shadows and *real* areas of reflected light.

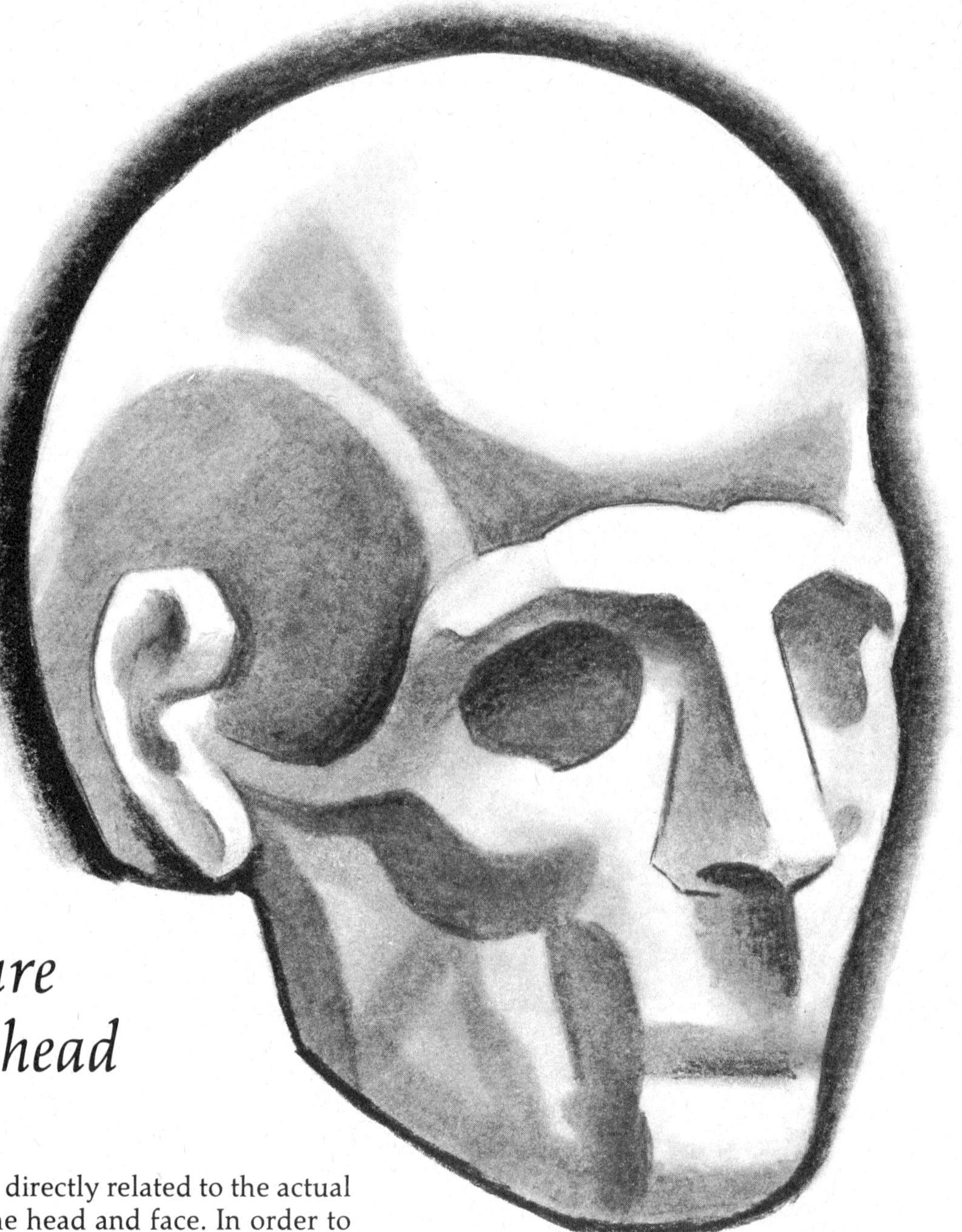

Structure of the head

All makeup is directly related to the actual structure of the head and face. In order to achieve the effects from your makeup work you must study the facial structure. The prominent high points of the bone masses in the structure of the head include the forehead, cheekbone, jawbone — as well as the cartilage of the nose, the eyeball of the eyesocket and the teeth.

Optical illusion

These illustrations clearly indicate the effects created by the discretionary interplay of light and dark to achieve optical illusion.

COLOUR GUIDE

Fashion today does not stop at the neck. The look continues — to the makeup. The way to think of makeup is that it is like an accessory; a very important one. Colour combinations are now being worn to create an exciting total look to complement your wardrobe.

You will learn in the basic principles section that the classic placement of eye colours are applied in three different shades. The brow bone shading being the deepest of the three, the lid colour being a medium shade and the highlighter, the lightest one of all. Your colour choice can be in monochromatic colour schemes, (using deeper and lighter shades of the same colour) or colours that complement each other.

When choosing eye colours, think in terms of complementing and enhancing the eyes or clothing, rather than feeling that you must match them. Do not limit your choice to following makeup colour guides that specify there are only certain colours suitable for your particular hair and eye colouring. Because of so many variables in hair, eye and skin shades, in addition to the many colour hues available in each tone of eye shadow it is difficult to follow any set ruling. Conversely, you will find some shades not recommended for your colouring to be extremely effective, e.g., a certain light shade of green may be totally wrong for you, whereas a smoky or muted tone of green may be just perfect and one of your most flattering colours.

As you experiment with different colours you will become aware of the shades that work best for you.

The following guides are but a few suggestions on colour variations suitable for different eye colouring — as mentioned previously do not limit your selection to only these colours.

Brown eyes

Most every colour as long as it is not bright. Deep smoky colours work best. Smoky plum, olive, charcoal, etc.

Hazel eyes

Muted greens, muted blue, aqua, plum, brown, gold, cinnamon, rust, copper, apricot, toast, olive and grey.

Green eyes

Plum, brown, muted blue, navy blue, aqua, gold, copper and rust.

Blue eyes

Soft heathery tones — lavender, grey, soft burgundy and plums, aqua, muted green, dusky pink, brown.

Colours suitable for all eye colouring

Grey, taupe and browns. These are good basic shades to work with no matter what your eye colouring is. The contrast of using brown tones on the eyes brings out the colour of the iris. One exception to using browns would be for a more mature woman with greying hair. Softer tones of blues, pale grey, and lavenders are much more flattering.

The following shadows are some good basics for any makeup wardrobe to enable you to change the tone of your eye shadows, thus giving you more flexibilities with shades you may already possess.

Black eye shadow can be one of your most versatile colours, depending upon the application techniques employed. Do not think of black as just stark "black" — it can be used alone to create a soft smokey effect, or to achieve stronger definition. It can also be used over any shade where a deeper tone is desired. e.g., you could use the same colour for shading the brow bone as used on the lid, by deepening with black to create a monochromatic tone. Dark brown or charcoal shades also work effectively in adding depth to lighter colours.

Cream, white or very pale colour tones may be used to lighten deeper colours — use under or over to change or soften the colour tone.

"Iridescent dusts" used in conjunction with flat shadows can achieve various degrees of pearlized effects. To achieve extra pearl or for softening and changing colour tones, use with any one of the eye shadows, including the creams. "Iridescent dusts" are also effective for highlighting the eyes or other areas of the face, in addition to mixing well with blushes and lipsticks when an iridescent glow is desired.

Lips and blush

Decide what you are going to wear and let your clothing guide your choice of lipstick shade.

The time of day should also be taken into consideration and carried through with all makeup. Keep in mind that artificial light drains colour and daylight accentuates colour.

The following colour suggestions will assist you in co-ordinating your lipstick shade with your clothing colours.

Browns, beiges, yellows and greens

Lipsticks should be in tones of bronze, peach, orange or shades with an underlying gold tone.

Blues and lavenders

Lipsticks in tones of pink or burgundy are most flattering.

Black and white

Amost any shade can be worn; the depth is important when wearing black as it is such a strong colour. Tones of red are most effective with black and white.

Red, pinks and orange

The best choice when wearing these definite colours is to match your lipstick shade accordingly.

Lip colour and blush should be in the same colour range . . . or you could stay in the same family but vary the tone, i.e. Burgundy lip colour looks wonderful with rose blush, but not peach. By the same token, raspberry tone blush would be wrong with a bronze lip colour.

Lip and blush should harmonize with other makeup colours used. Colour depth should balance — a strong eye makeup should be carried through with a deeper shade of lip colour — a softer eye makeup would be balanced with a lighter lip shade.

CORRECTIVE TECHNIQUES

Basic face shapes and corrective facial contouring

If you have difficulty analysing your face shape, it is due to the fact that there are so many variations of each face shape.

The seven basic shapes are oval, round, oblong, triangle (or pear), heart (or inverted triangle), square and diamond. Most face shapes cannot be categorized perfectly. However, a face will usually resemble one of the basic outlines, even though it may have some of the characteristics of another.

The illustrations and guidelines that follow will give you a better idea of the face shape nearest your own. It is important that you understand, in relating to your particular face shape, that it does not always mean you should apply corrective contouring if you don't happen to have that perfect "oval". Many of the face shapes mentioned are most attractive in their own right. The corrective contouring is intended for those face shapes that are too obviously extreme in shape to create a sense of balance with the facial features.

Oval

The classic, perfectly proportioned face is balanced both horizontally and vertically. It is made up of three equal parts horizontally, and five equal parts vertically.

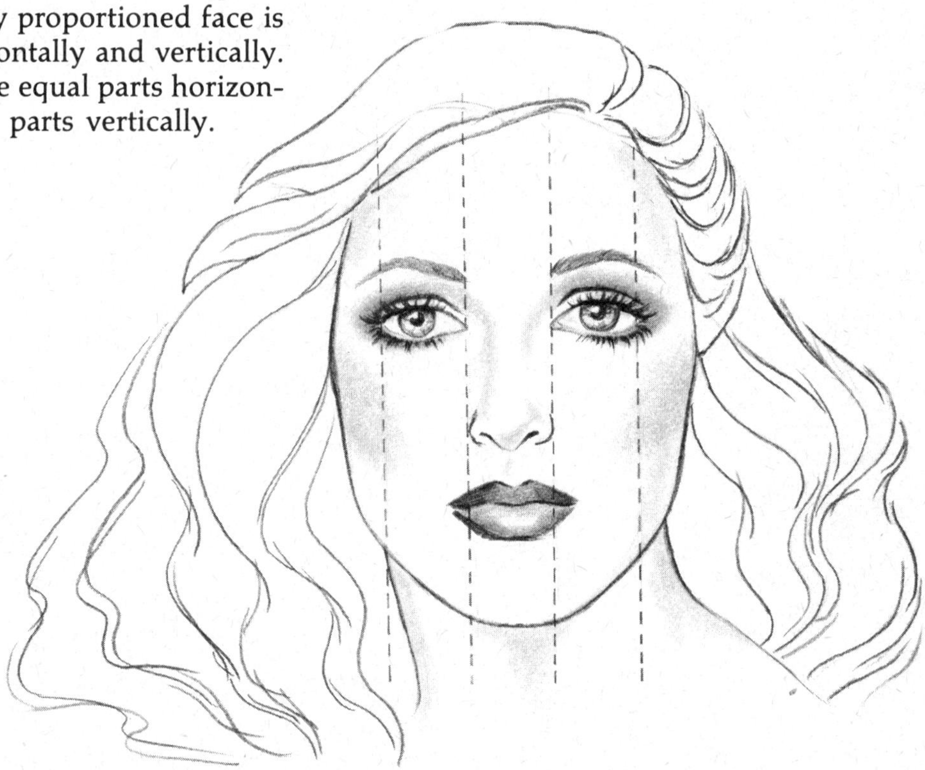

Round

The typical marks are full cheeks, a rounded jawline and very often a rounded hairline.

CORRECTIVE PROCEDURE: Shade along the sides of the forehead, the temples and the sides of the face. Be sure to avoid the shaded section when applying blush.

Oblong

The face is usually long and angular with fairly straight lines.

CORRECTIVE PROCEDURE: Shade the upper portion of the forehead and the area along the jawline.

Square

The forehead and the jawline are almost equal in width. The sides of the face are generally angular.

CORRECTIVE PROCEDURE: Shade the jawline from the bottom of the ears, down to and including the chin.

Diamond

The forehead and chin are narrow; the cheekbones are wide.

CORRECTIVE PROCEDURE: Shade the temples and cheekbone area (the widest part of the face), plus the sharp angle of the chin. Highlight the sides of the forehead and the jawline from the back of the jawbone to the chin.

Triangle (or pear)

The forehead is narrow and the jawline is wider than the cheekbones.

CORRECTIVE PROCEDURE: Shade the full jawline starting at the bottom of the ears down to where the chin begins. Highlight the narrow sides of the forehead including the temples.

Heart (or inverted triangle)

The forehead is wide and the cheekbones prominent, the jaws and chin are narrow.

CORRECTIVE PROCEDURE: Shade the wide sides of the forehead including the temples. Round the chin by shading its lower dimension. Highlight the jawline from the bottom of the ears to the shaded chin.

Thin
To "widen" apply highlighter to the outer areas from the temple down to the jawline.

Hollow
Use a light shadow in the hollows. Eliminate completely regular cheekbone shading.

Receding chin

A triangle of light shadow over the chin which is brought from a point just below the lip and extended along the jawline to a point halfway from the chin to the ear will bring out the chin.

Double chin

Apply shading just under jawbone, blend from ear to ear along the jawline and under the chin.

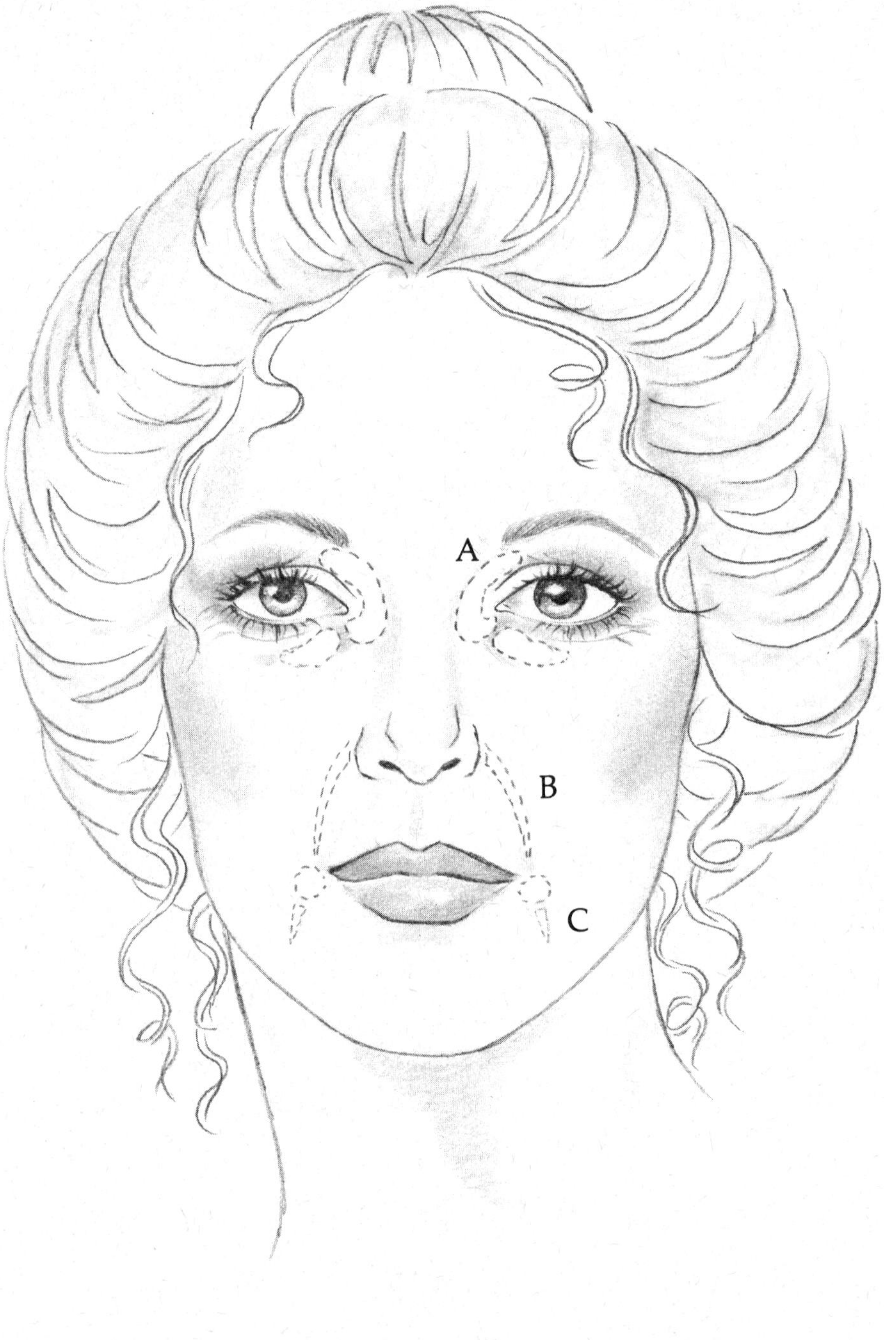
A
B
C

Aging areas to correct by highlighting

A. The area between the edge of the bridge of the nose and the inside corner of the eye tends to have a sunken appearance with age. Highlight this area to counteract the depth. Do not apply eye shading to this area as you will only exaggerate the problem. Start the shading further out.

B. The crease that forms around the outer areas of the nostrils, moving down to the outside corner of the mouth can be softened by applying highlighting directly into the crease line.

C. In the aging process, small indentations sometimes develop just below the outside corners of the mouth. Another crease often forms from this indentation running down to the chin.

These shadow areas add age to the appearance of the face. By highlighting, you create the illusion of bringing these areas out of the shadows, softening and making them less noticeable. Correct blending is crucial. Use the touch and press technique to eliminate demarcation and to avoid moving the "light" away from the specific area of placement.

Correcting the nose

Corrective techniques in contouring the nose can create the illusion of a better proportion or size of the nose. As with all corrective procedures, care should be taken to effect the illusion without the results being obvious.

Thin

Highlight both sides of the nose and if necessary, augment that by shading the tip to create a somewhat shorter and therefore wider appearance.

Broad

Shade both sides of the nose starting at the bridge, extending downward to the sides of the nostrils. Highlight in a narrow line down the middle.

Long

Apply shading to the edge of the nostrils and under the tip.

Short and turned up

To create more length, shade both sides of the nose, starting at the bridge and extending down the sides of the nostrils. Highlight in a narrow line down the middle. If the end of the nose is turned up, (pug), shade this area to flatten.

Hooked

Shade the actual hook or bent area and highlight directly above and below.

Crooked

Shade the side of the nose that is crooked. With a highlighter, draw a narrow, straight line down the length of the nose starting from the bridge to the tip, paying no attention to where the middle of the nose actually lies but creating a new, symmetrical illusion.

High at the bridge

Blend a darker shade down the bridge of the nose and a lighter shade down each side.

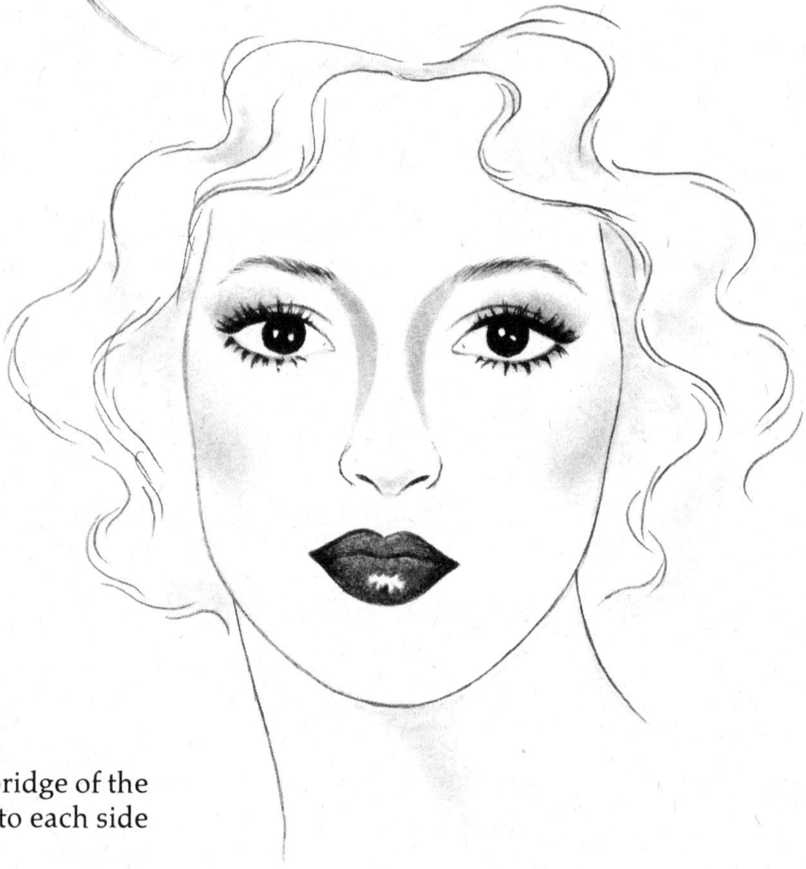

Wide across the bridge

One can alter the width of the bridge of the nose by applying a dark shade to each side of the bridge.

Correcting the eyes

Before applying eye makeup, it is important to study your eye shape in order to determine if you require special instruction that varies from the basic principles of eye makeup in colour variance or placement.

The following guidelines apply to eye shapes most often requiring corrective procedures, enabling you to make the most of your eyes regardless of their size or shape.

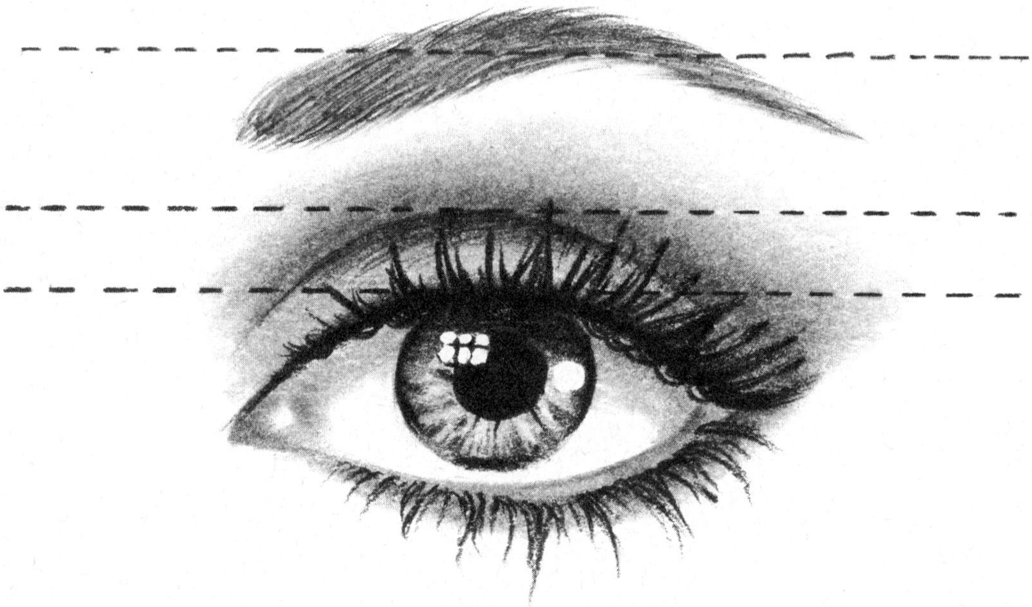

A well-balanced eye can be measured using these approximate ratios. The area from the root of the lash to the crease of the eye is one-half that of the area between the crease of the eye and the brow at its peak.

Wide-set

Goal — to bring closer together. Start all of the application close to the nose and stop before reaching the outer corner of the eye.

Close-set

Goal — to separate. Create the illusion of more space by beginning the eye shading slightly back from the corner of the eye and extending beyond the outer corner. Using a very light shadow on the inner corner and blending into a deeper tone is also very effective.

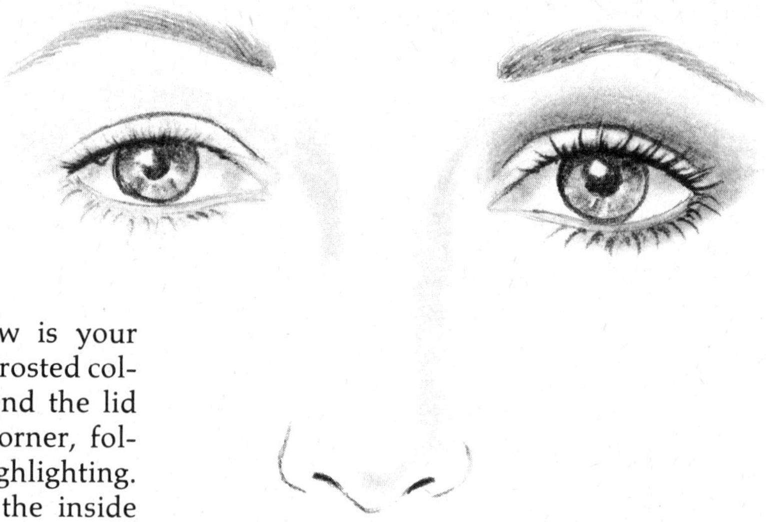

Small

Goal — to open. Dark shadow is your enemy. Use only light pastel or frosted colours on the lid to amplify. Blend the lid colour out beyond the outer corner, following with the shading and highlighting. Apply a light-toned pencil to the inside rim of the lower eyelid.

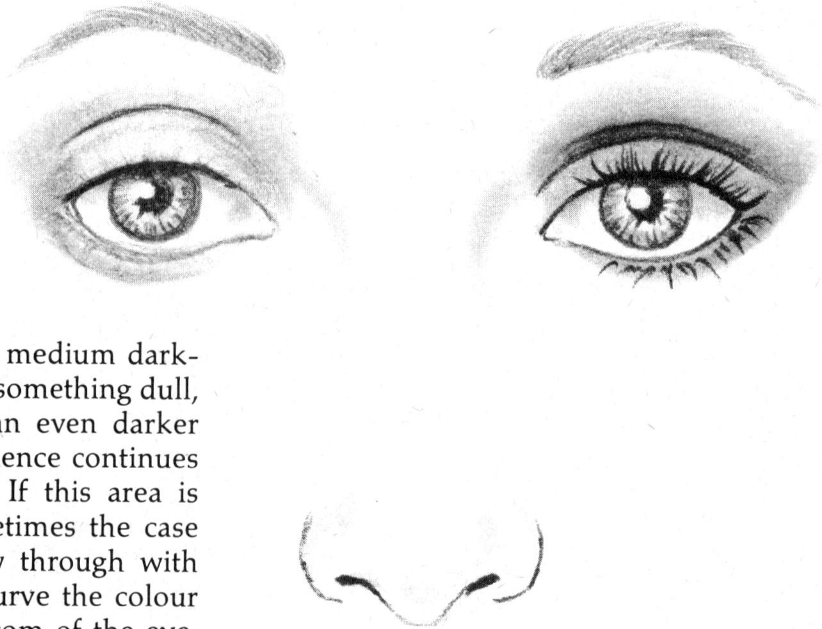

Bulging

Goal — to flatten. Apply a medium dark-toned colour to the eyelid, something dull, deep and muted. Apply an even darker tone for shading if prominence continues up into the orbital bone. If this area is somewhat flat, (as is sometimes the case with bulging eyes), follow through with the lid colour to shade. Curve the colour around just under the bottom of the eye, especially if there is any protrusion in that area. Do not use pale frosted or glossy shadows. Apply a charcoal, coal, or deep-toned soft pencil to both the upper and the lower inside rims of the eyelids.

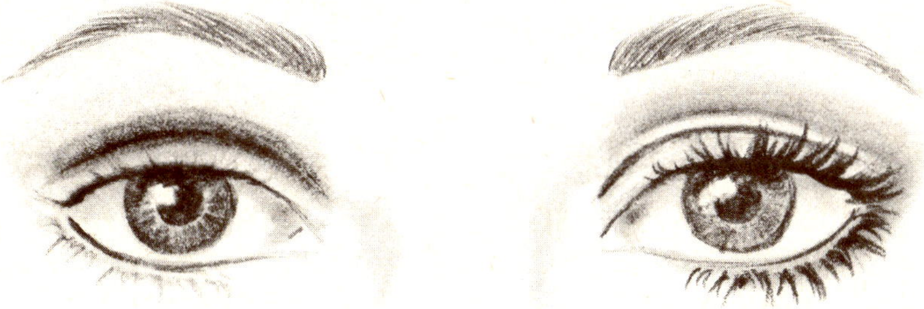

Deep-set

Goal — to bring forward. Apply a lid colour which is light and bright to optically "pull" the eye forward. The colour should extend up into the natural crease of the eye. Apply shading to the area directly above the natural crease following with highlighter.

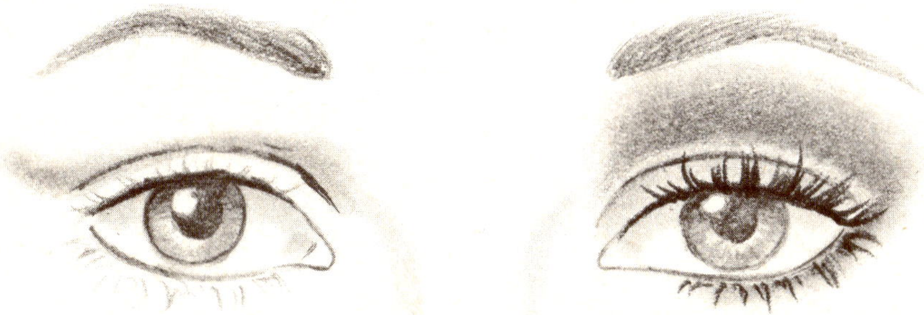

Prominent brow bone

Goal — to recede. When the strength of the orbital bone overpowers the eyes, the area from above the crease to the brow bone should be receded, to give it less importance. Select a shade that is deep, flat and dull — bright or frosted shades cannot be used. If the area directly under the brow is prominent too, (often referred to as an "over-hanging" brow), apply a medium-toned shadow to optically "push" it back, rather than a very light tone generally used for highlighting.

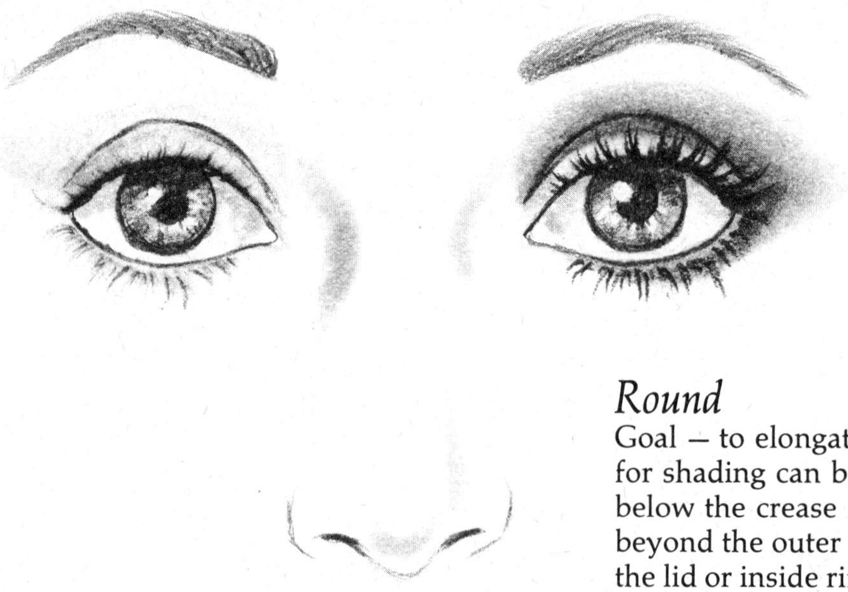

Round

Goal — to elongate. The eye shadow used for shading can be brushed down slightly below the crease line. Extend all shadows beyond the outer corner of the eye. Apply the lid or inside rim lining to the outer half of the eye.

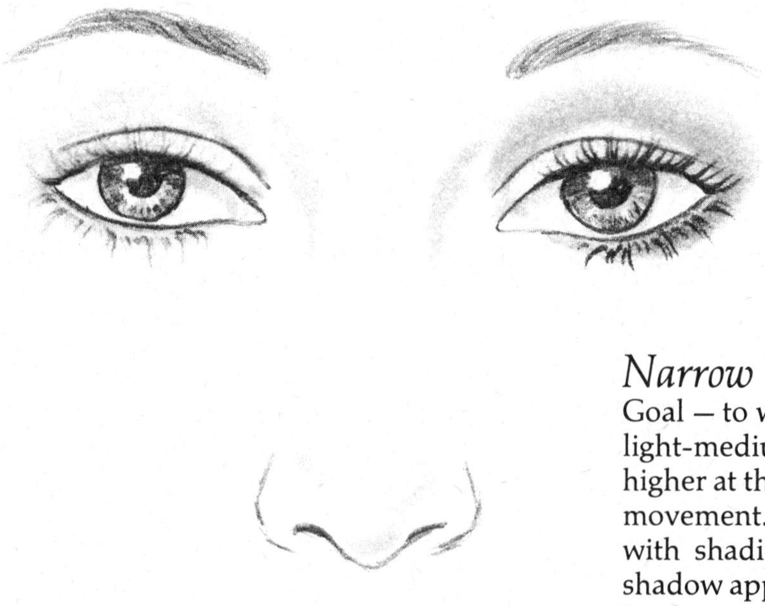

Narrow Almond

Goal — to widen. Apply a lid colour that is light-medium. Extend the colour slightly higher at the centre of the eye in a rounded movement. Follow this corrected shape with shading and highlighting. A lighter shadow applied to the centre area of the lid is also very effective to achieve a wider appearance to the eyes.

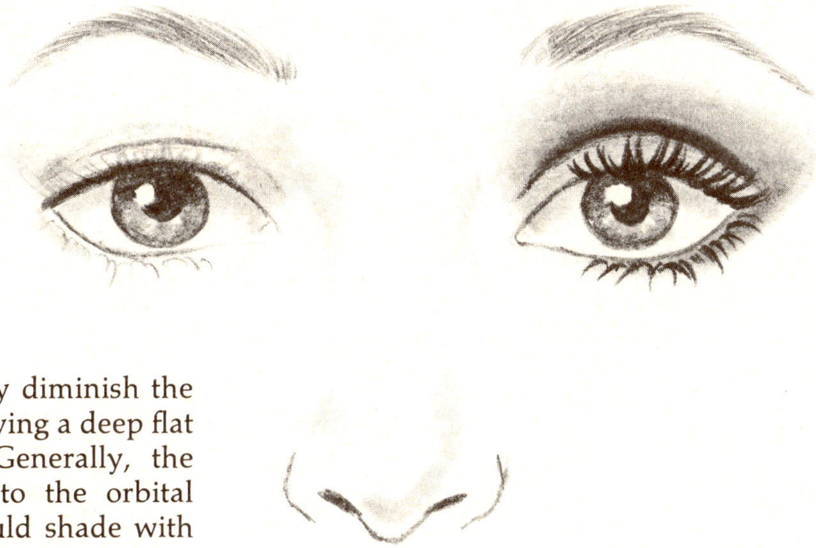

Puffy lids

Goal — to reduce. Optically diminish the puffiness on the lid by applying a deep flat muted tone of shadow. Generally, the puffy lid continues up into the orbital bone. In this case you would shade with only flat dark muted tones of brown. A darker concentration of shadow can be applied for extra depth in the crease if necessary.

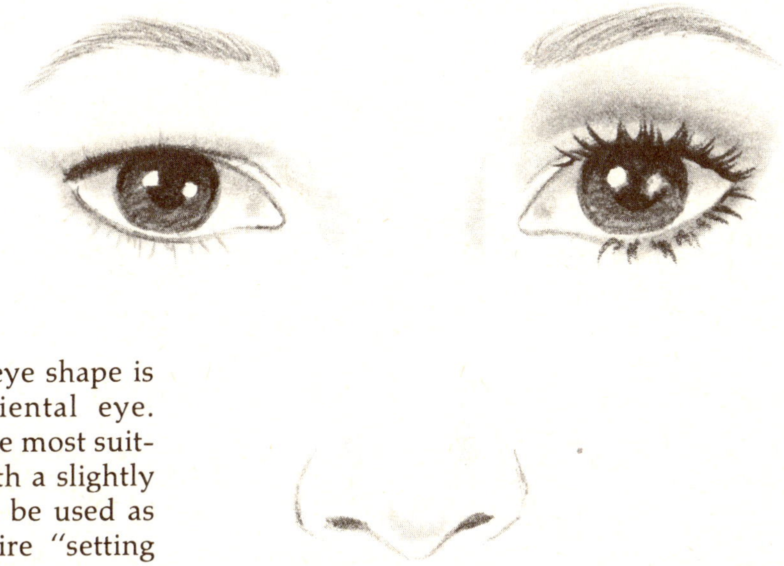

Flat

Goal — to create depth. This eye shape is most common with the oriental eye. Deeper, more muted shades are most suitable for lid shadow. Shade with a slightly deeper tone. Warm tones can be used as this eye type does not require "setting back" in the frontal bone area. Create depth and definition by applying a dark shade to the eye socket (the normal crease area).

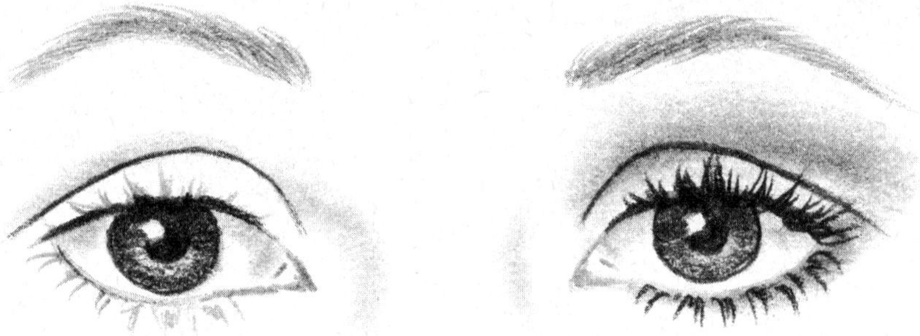

Drooping eye lid

Goal — to lift. Start the shading narrow at the inner corner, widen it in an upward slant toward the outer corner of the eye. For drooping crease line, optically lift the sagging lid by applying deeper shadow to the area one imagines existed before the droop. If the droop is extensive at the outer corner, stop all the shading and outlining short of the corners of the eye.

Crepey

Goal — not to emphasize. Use soft colours and a light hand. Heavy application, bright, bold colours and highly frosted shadows will only accentuate the problem. Outlining the eyes will give more emphasis or a more dramatic look. Use muted tones, dark stark colours would appear too harsh.

Correcting the lips

It is not practical to make a drastic change in altering your lip shape, however, clever use of correct colour and outline can improve the contours of the mouth and hide little imperfections. Any corrective procedures used should be very subtle, with any degree of change being only the slightest amount inside or outside the natural lip line. The principle of light and dark also comes into play when correcting the lips . . . light colours enlarge; dark or tawny shades reduce.

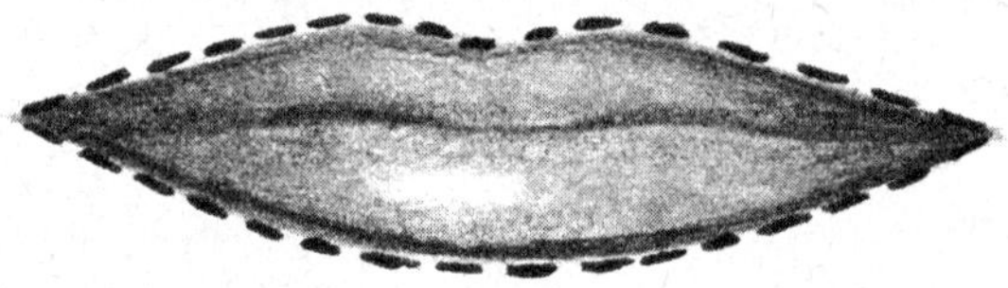

Thin

Trace around the outside of the natural lip line using a deep shade of lip pencil. Fill in with a bright, light lipstick. Avoid using any dark lip colours. Apply lip sheen to further emphasize.

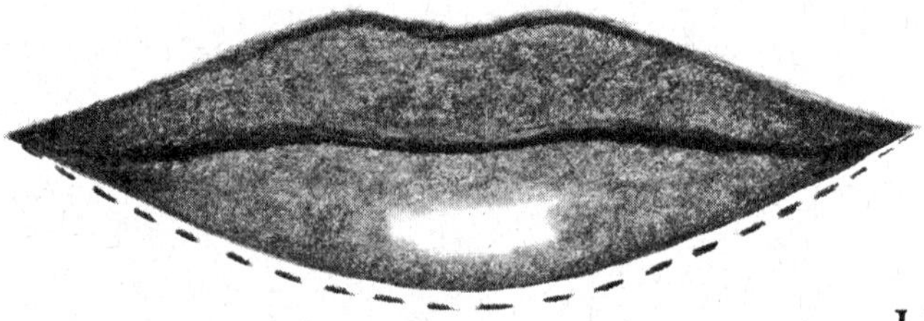

Unbalanced — thin bottom.

Magnify the lower lip by lining on the outside of the lip. Trace the outline of the top proportioned lip on its natural rim.

Unbalanced — thin top.

Reverse description for thin bottom. To further augment and emphasize, try:

a) Using two different shades of lipstick; the brighter, lighter one on the thinner lip.

b) Use one shade of lipstick and apply lip sheen . . . but to the thin lip only.

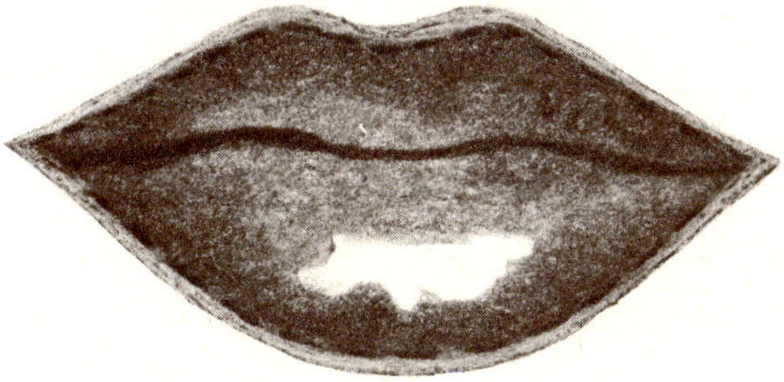

Full
Trace the shape of the lips just inside the natural line. Fill in with medium to dark shade. Do not use gloss or frosted shades.

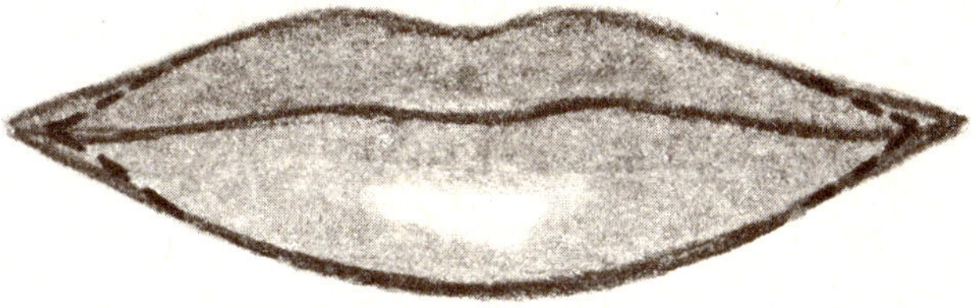

Wide
Outline the lips, creating new corners inside outer edge of lips. If lip sheen is used concentrate application to centre area only.

Down-turned at corners
Outline the lips to add a hint of a smile, by applying lip pencil slightly above lip shape at the outer corners of the top lip, and inside lip shape in the bottom corners.

How to create prettier lips

1. Using a lip pencil, draw tiny dots on the upper lip at the highest point of the natural bow.
2. Place another dot inside the *centre* of the bow approximately a quarter of the way in from the lip line to the bottom of the upper lip.
3. Draw two more dots just fractionally above the outside corners of the mouth.
4. Now connect the dots as illustrated using the same lip pencil.
5. Outline the bottom lip following the natural curvature of the mouth moving slightly in on the outer corners to line up with the upper outline.
6. Apply lip colour to fill in, blending into the lip pencil so that the lip outline is not obvious.

These steps will give a more defined shape to the bow, and the slight raising of the corners will give a pleasant expression to the mouth.

FLORENCE

DOROTHY

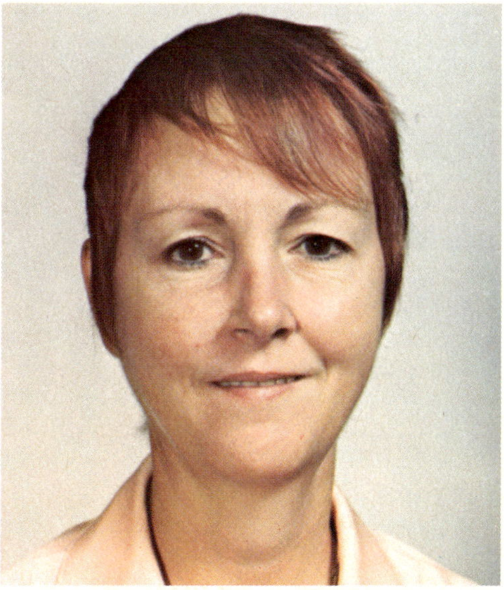

NANCY

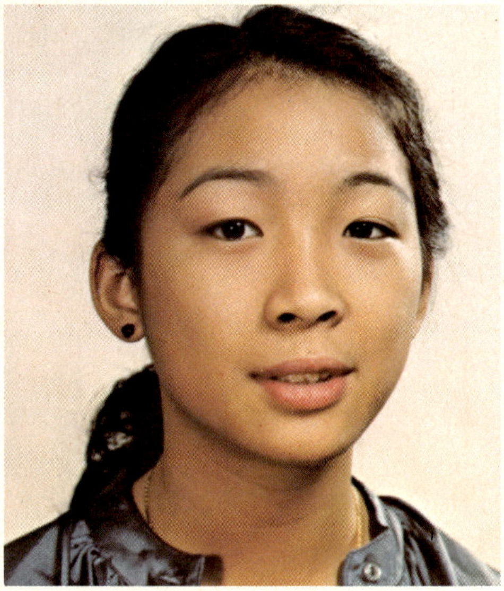

PARIS

JANET

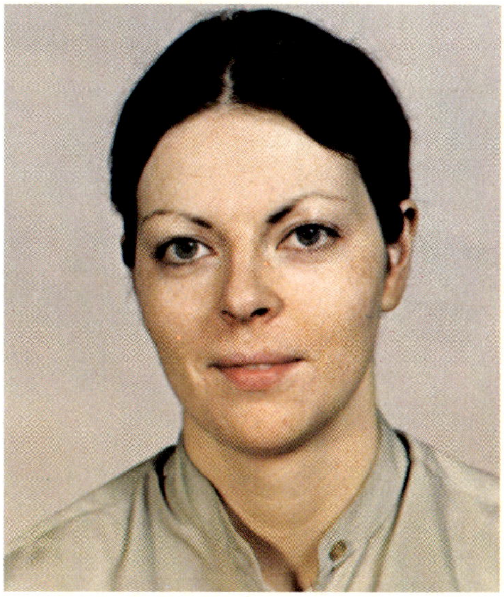

HELEN

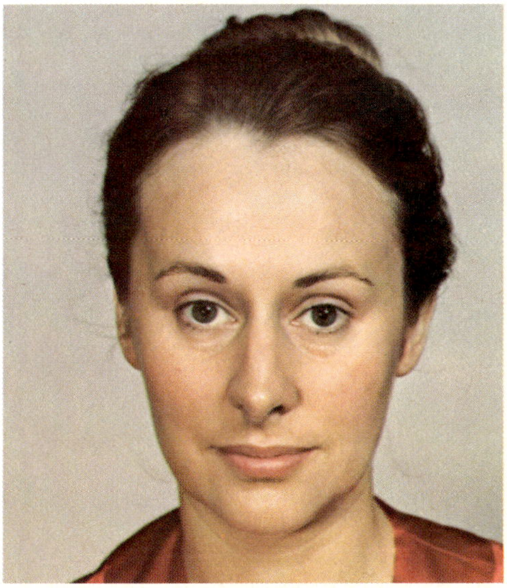

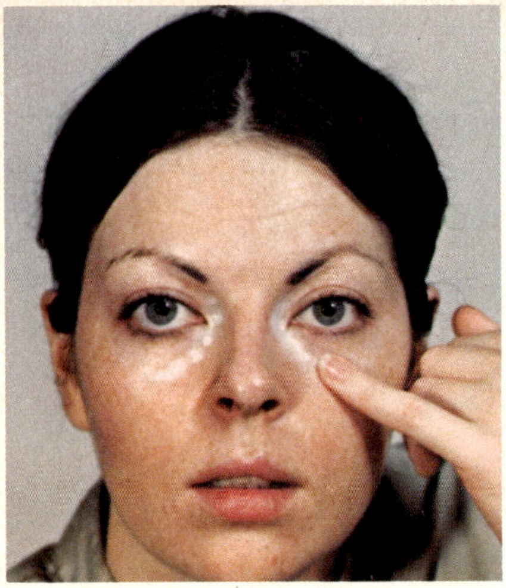

Scene I

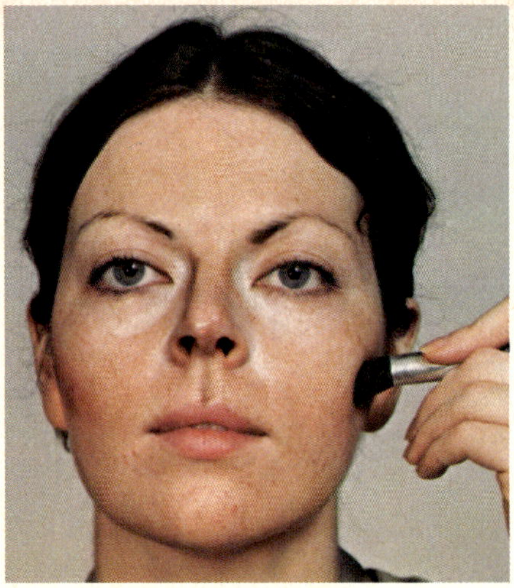

Scene II

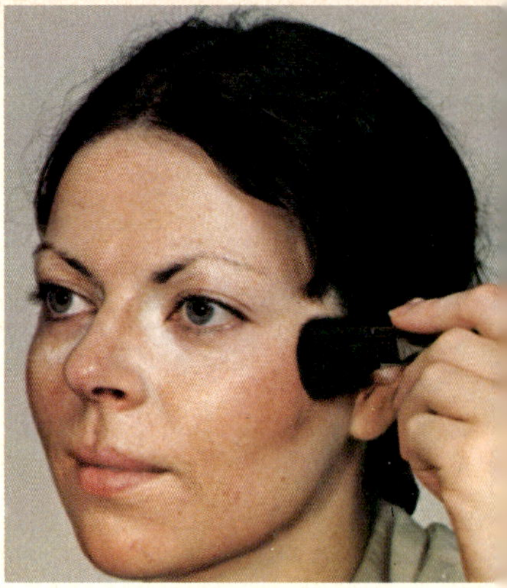

Scene III

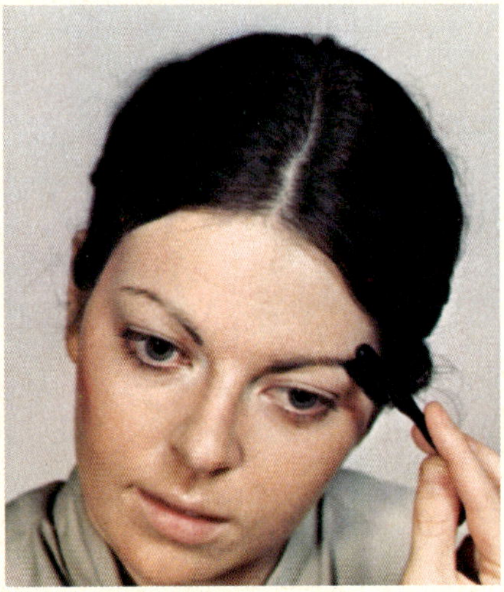

Scene VII

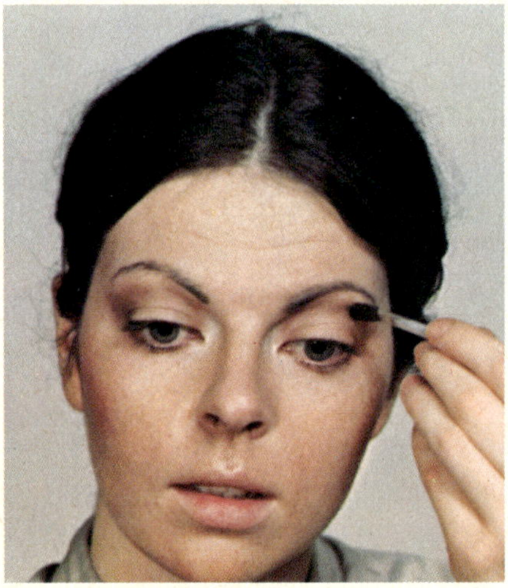

Scene VIII

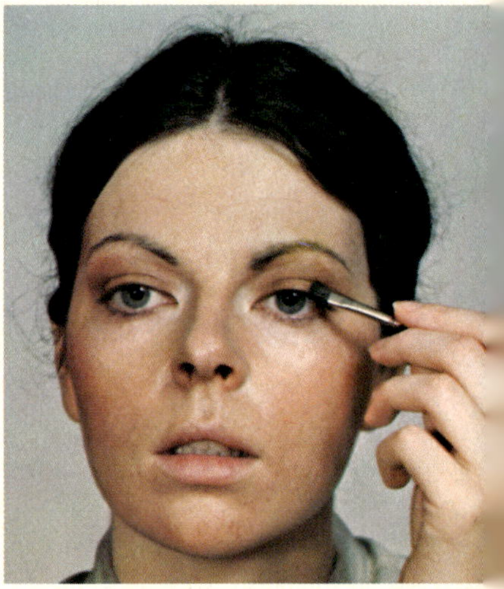

Scene IX

Scene XI

Scene XII

Scene XIII

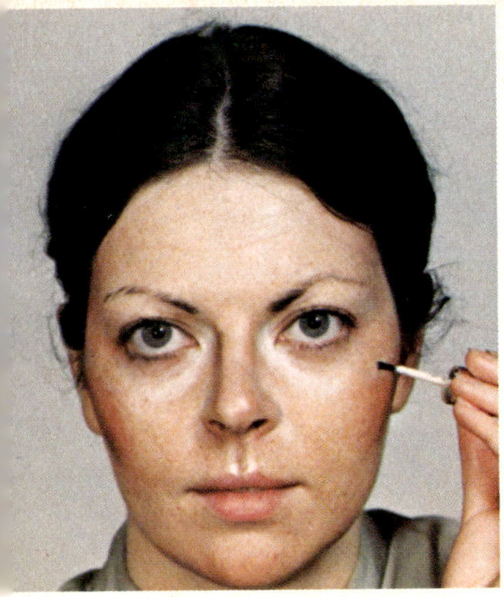

Scene IV

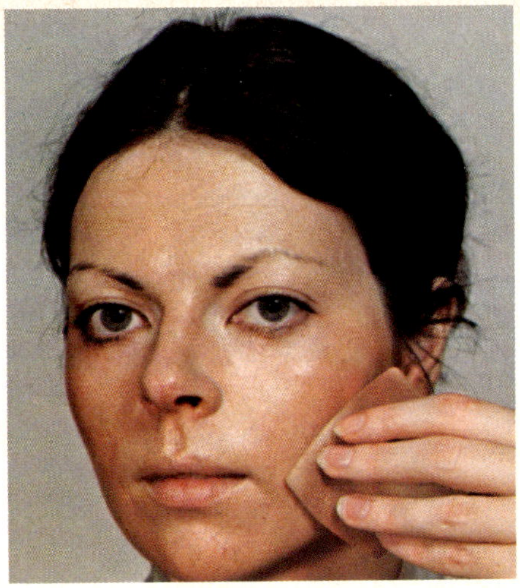

Scene V

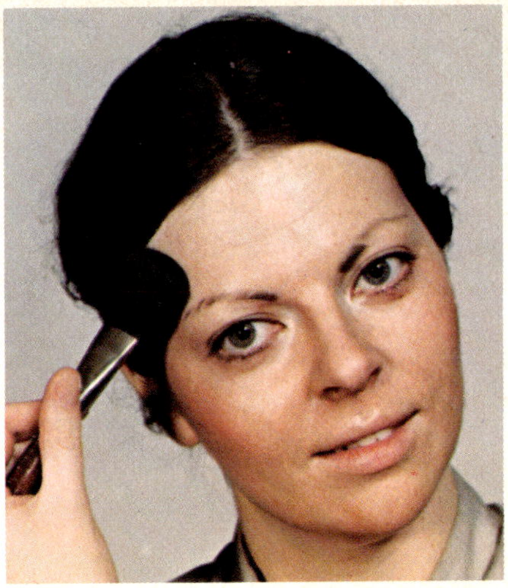

Scene VI

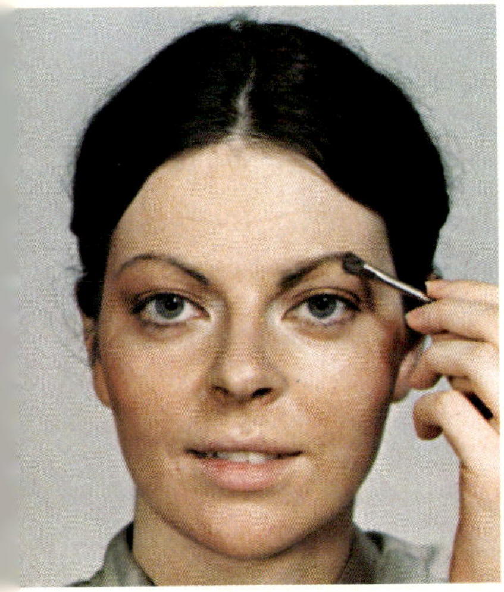

Scene X

Scene XIII

Scene XIV

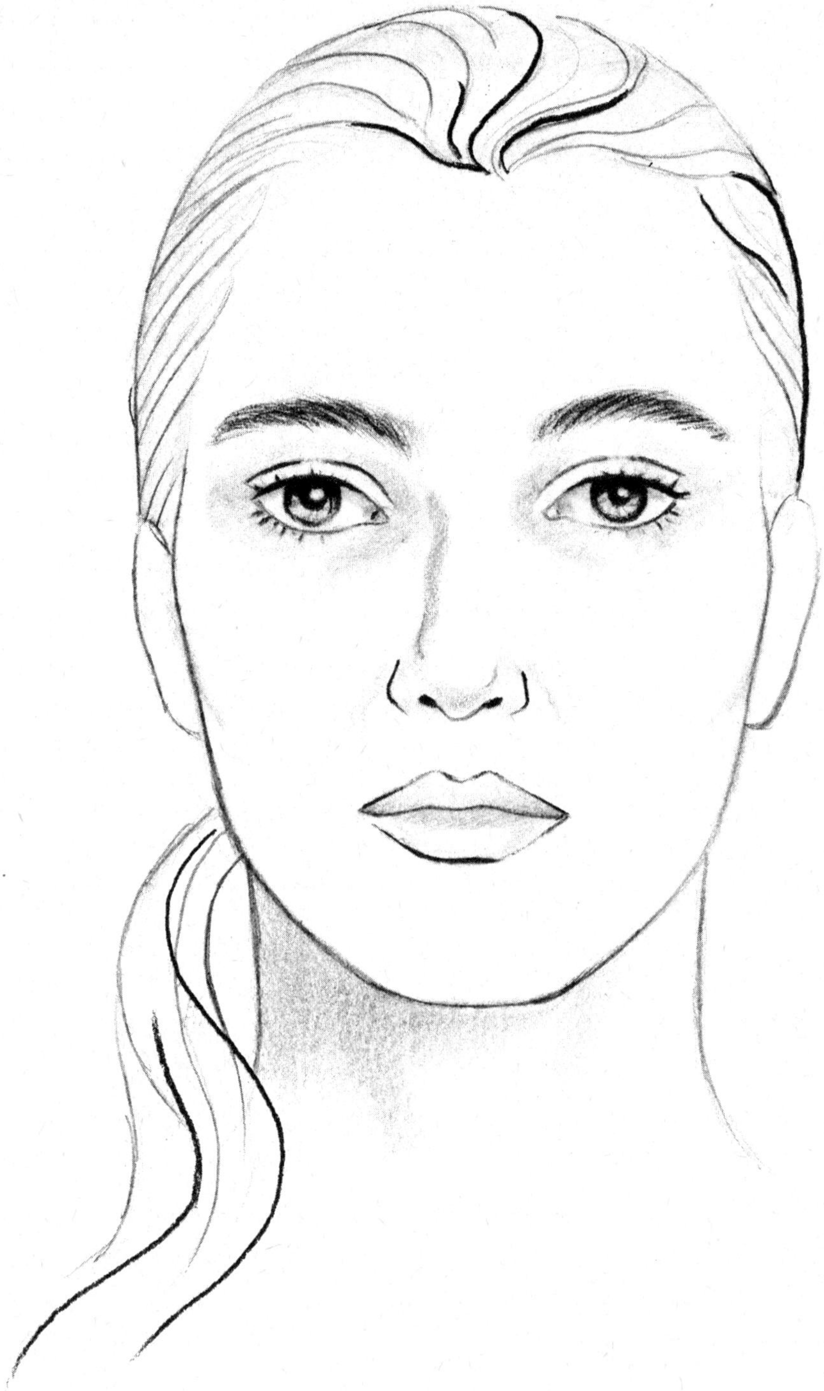

THE BASIC PRINCIPLE OF MAKEUP ARTISTRY

Before discussing the makeup techniques we should consider the canvas on which it is to be applied. Makeup application must always begin on a clean healthy-looking skin. Understanding and taking care of your skin is of the utmost importance. Makeup can certainly do wonders in enhancing your natural beauty potential, but there is a limit to what you can hide. Nutrition, rest and exercise are all contributing factors to a radiant healthy skin, in addition to a skin care routine being as habitual as brushing your teeth.

The majority of the "Scenes" in "THE BASIC PRINCIPLE OF MAKEUP ARTISTRY" are timeless and will stay with you over the years without altering, because these techniques are based on the natural facial structure.

Using the simple philosophy of light colours bringing emphasis to an area, and dark matte colours introducing an illusion of shadow that make an area recede, you can work with your natural facial contours to minimize flaws and dramatize with shading, and to focus on your good points with highlighting.

Once you have learned the basic principles you will be able to easily adapt to makeup variations to keep up with current fashion trends. Use as many or as few of these makeup steps as you feel comfortable with, and always remember that your clothes and makeup should complement each other, creating total harmony. Like an artist at work, you should know how much colour to apply to the canvas of your face. Obviously, you shouldn't wear full evening makeup when you are in the sun. The main change for evening makeup is to use stronger colours and to increase the intensity of the application, keeping in mind that artificial light drains colour, while daylight accentuates.

As we move from "Scene I" through "Scene XIV" you will observe the gradual changes, as our illustrator builds and structures the facial features to guide your application. Understanding the facial structuring and putting into practice the techniques of makeup artistry will enable you to make the most of your individual beauty.

Scene I

Concealer

Concealing cream is designed to give extra cover to specific areas of the face. Primarily a concealer is used to diminish dark circles, but it is also useful for hiding blemishes, broken capillaries, brown spots and other areas of discolouration. A concealer can also be effective in diminishing aging facial creases.

APPLICATION PROCEDURE: To cover "dark circles" under the eyes, apply concealer to semi-circle area only. Include coverage to the inner eye area and up into the side of the nose if necessary. Do not continue around under the outer half of the eye, (a mistake commonly made), as circles very rarely continue any further than halfway. As tiny lines form in the outer eye area, any build up of cream or extra coverage tends to emphasize these lines.

Apply concealer, sparsely dotting the area with a small sponge applicator or Q-tip. Turn to a clean end, or using your little finger, dab and pat until the cream is blended evenly and smoothly. Pay particular attention to creating a thin screen while maintaining a good cover. The area should remain shades lighter than the surrounding area.

To conceal blemishes and other areas of discolouration, apply to specific area requiring coverage, and blend edges carefully.

For covering facial creases, apply concealer with an eyeliner brush to the indentation. Blend carefully, making sure the cream is contained within the crease.

Scene II

Facial Shading

By shading the face, you can correct and minimize facial flaws in addition to creating an illusion of shadow, depth or definition to specific areas.

Facial shading can be achieved by using a brown-toned pressed powder shadow, cream, or a darker tone of foundation. The type of product you use is a matter of personal choice. Your natural skin tone determines the depth of tone you would require.

A. Cheek bone

The first step in creating the illusion of higher cheekbones is achieved by shading under the cheekbone to optically deepen the hollow.

APPLICATION PROCEDURE: First of all it is important to determine the correct placement of cheek shading. To do this, you must feel for the natural hollow of your cheekbone, or you can also determine placement by sucking in the cheeks for visual guidance.

A contour brush should be used for shading with powder, a sponge being more suitable for cream or foundation application.

Apply the shading directly below the cheekbone, starting at an imaginary line running down from the outer corner of the iris. Blend outward following the underline of the bone. The natural bone structure will guide your application in a diagonal line generally finishing even with the lower section of the earlobe.

B. Chin and jawline

Shading can be used to optically deepen the natural shadow beneath the *chin* and *jawbone* to achieve a more structured jawline. It can also be used to minimize fleshiness or a double chin, as well as define and add depth to a shallow chin or jaw.

C. Nose and philtrum

If you wish to give a more sculptured or finely chiselled effect to the nose, or more definition to the *philtrum* (centre valley above the upper lip) and the indentation below the bottom lip, follow through with shading in these areas.

APPLICATION PROCEDURE: For shading the jawline, a contour brush should be used for powder application, and a sponge for cream or foundation.

Start the application directly under the chin, blend back along the jawline to the ear. Confine shading to the natural indentation. Do not continue down in to the neck area.

For the nose, use a #8 shading brush. Shade both sides of the nose starting at the bridge extending downward to the sides of the nostrils. For nostril definition, shade the indentation of the nostril with an eyeliner brush. Using the shading brush, define the philtrum, from below the nose down to the lip directly inside the centre of the valley. Follow with shading into the natural indentation below the lip.

All shading can be applied with definition at this stage. The combination with foundation application covered in Scene V affects the end result of shading when using this technique of application.

Scene III

Cheek colour

Cheek colour is used to give the cheek bones more emphasis and to create a radiant natural glow of vitality and health to the face. This application is an important element in brightening the entire face.

Blush is available in cream and powder formulas, flat finish and pearlized for extra glow. The choice of colour should be determined in part by your skin tone. A tanned or darker complexion requires stronger shades; basically any shade can be used on a medium skin tone, and pale skin is best with softer blush tones. Don't be timid in selecting tones of red. Bright colours do not appear as definite when applied onto the skin. Red can be worn on any skin tone, however, the intensity of the application will vary.

Remember, the colour of the blush you select should co-ordinate with your lipstick shade.

APPLICATION PROCEDURE: A rouge brush is most effective for pressed powder application. Cream may be applied with a foam sponge or the fingertips.

The placement of cheek colour is constant — on the *cheek bone.* Use the outside corner of the iris as a guide for where to start this application. Do not start the colour any closer to the nose as it will not only draw attention to the nose but also emphasize the rounded fleshy area of the cheek which in turn detracts from the cheekbone itself. Blend out toward the hairline following the natural curve of the bone. The colour applied should blend into the shading to eliminate a line of separation between the two colours. Avoid applying colour upward towards the eye. In most cases this type of application looks unnatural and can also detract from the eyes in addition to emphasizing little crow's feet. This step can be used for high fashion but is not suitable for everyone.

Two of the most common mistakes women make in applying makeup is putting the blush in the wrong place, and not blending correctly to avoid demarcation lines. Keep in mind that your natural bone structure should guide your application.

The end result after Scene V will give the appearance of a natural warm glow, as opposed to a stark artificial effect.

The colour may also be brushed very lightly onto the temples, the tip of the chin, and beneath the ear lobes to create a healthy blush. This is very flattering for a woman who has lost the natural glow to her face.

Scene IV

Facial highlighting

Highlight can be used to further augment the height of the cheek bone.

A lighter tone creates an optical illusion of the cheek bone being so extended that the light catches on the top and cannot get beyond. Highlight may also be applied to the nose, chin, and philtrum to give added definition.

Highlighters are available in flat or pearlized formulas, in pressed powder shadow, liquid or cream. A light flesh tone or cream colour is suitable for light to medium skin tones. For a darker complexion, choose a product a few shades lighter than your foundation.

APPLICATION PROCEDURE: Start the application at the same imaginary line you used for shading and colour application. Using a small flat-edged shadow brush, apply the highlighter in a narrow diagonal line on the crest of the cheek bone, directly above the cheek colour. Blend the two colours to avoid any line of separation.

To complete contouring of the nose apply the highlight down the centre in a straight even line. Carefully blend edges.

To further define the philtrum, highlight each side of the valley that runs from the lip up to the nose.

Apply highlight to the chin in a rounded shape below the indentation of the lip and above where the chin moves forward.

Scene V

Foundation Application

The purposes of using a foundation are to create an all over even facial tone, to cover imperfections and give the face the illusion of having smoother skin texture.

To select the correct shade of foundation, match as closely as possible to your natural skin tone. A foundation should be like your second skin, blending with your natural colouring. Two exceptions would be: using a warm rosy foundation to brighten a sallow complexion, and a beige foundation to tone down the high colouring of a ruddy complexion.

Your choice of a foundation formula is determined in part by the condition of your skin. A liquid foundation provides a sheer transparent cover suitable for normal skin in good condition and a cream formula provides more coverage.

APPLICATION PROCEDURE: For best results use a foam or natural sea sponge. The sponge is important in achieving a smooth, even application. Often when using fingertips, the majority of women tend to apply too much foundation and excessive pressure to the skin.

Apply the foundation directly onto the sponge, or dot onto the forehead, nose, cheeks and chin. Always use soft, light strokes with this application. *Never rub or pull the skin.* The objective is to blend *onto* the skin not *into* it. Proceed to blend, starting at the forehead, working out, then down the sides of the temple. Pat around the eye area from the outer to inner corner using a gentle touch, including the eyelids. Blend down and out onto the nose area. Continue the application working up and out from the chin towards the hairline to cover the balance of the face. The foundation should also be applied to the lips. Carefully blend the foundation off, down under the chin and jawline, to avoid any lines of demarcation.

Correct blending is particularly important in the makeup steps, as all facial contouring is applied prior to the foundation. The effect should be a natural veil allowing the shadow and highlight to show through. This method makes it possible for even the novice makeup artist to define and structure the facial features with professional results, thus achieving natural looking shades and highlights with very little effort.

There are few complexions of perfect uniform tone, however, if you are one of the fortunate few who really does not require a foundation, the utmost care must be taken if facial contouring is used.

For best results, start the application with a small amount of the product, gradually building up to a natural depth of application. Blend edges very carefully. Lines of demarcation should never be observed. It may take many hours of practice to perfect colour depth and correct blending to achieve believable results. Cream products are recommended for a more natural finish if a foundation is not used.

Scene VI

Powder application

Powder is used to set the foundation and provide a longer lasting matte finish. The invisible "veil" gives an overall soft velvety appearance to the skin and helps prevent a shiny build-up usually noticeable down the centre T-zone area of the face.

A loose colourless powder with a fine translucent texture should be used for best results. The colourless powder does not change the colour of the foundation or rouge and can be used on any skin tone.

APPLICATION PROCEDURE: Using a powder brush is the only truly effective method of powder application. A puff holds too much powder to be effective and cotton balls have a tendency to leave fine threads of fuzz behind. To apply, pick up small amounts of powder each time. Then shake off the excess before brushing it onto the face. Proceed, starting at the forehead, brushing with light downward strokes over the face, covering the eyes and lips as well. Be careful to avoid powder build-up particularly in the eye area as this will emphasize the tiny lines that form around the outer eye. Too much powder will also exaggerate crepiness on a more mature skin. If the powder is visible you have applied too much, or have not brushed it onto the skin correctly. When loose powder is properly applied, you will never have the appearance of a dull- or powdered-looking skin.

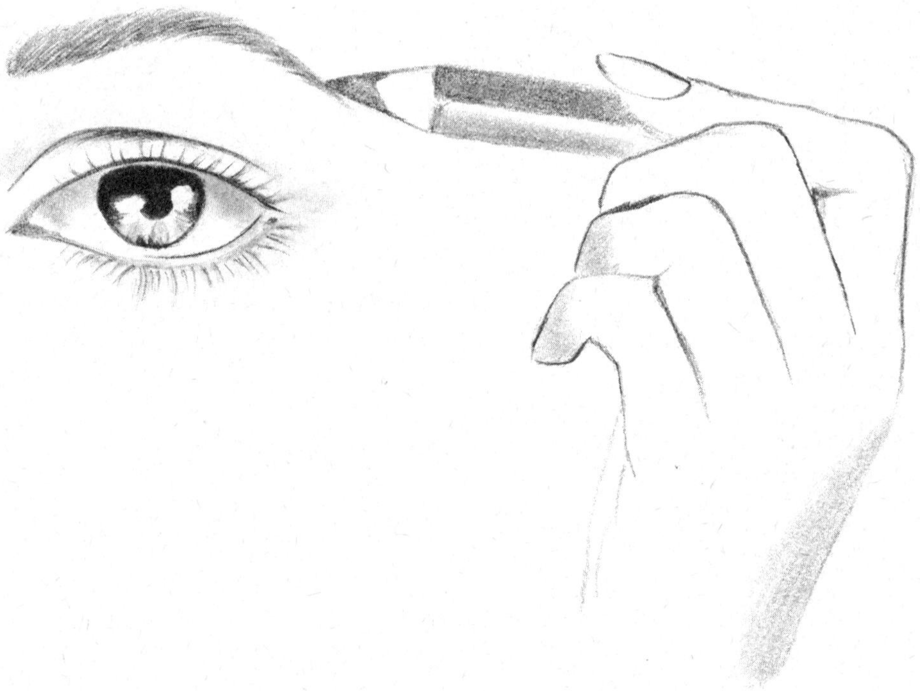

Scene VII

Eye brows

Brow makeup is used to colour, define, and correct the shape of the brow.

A pressed powder is best for deepening or lightening the shade of the brow. To correct the shape and fill in bare patches, a pencil is the most effective method. It is important to always keep the pencil sharp enough to simulate the natural hairs. A pressed powder shadow can also be used, moistened and applied with an eyeliner brush to create the same effect. However, you may need some practice to perfect this method.

The colour of the brows should be soft in relation to your hair and skin tone. If the brows are too dark, they overpower the face and detract from all the other features.

GENERAL RULE: If your hair is dark, the brows should be a shade or two lighter. If your hair is pale blonde, apply brow makeup a shade darker in order to make the brow visible enough to frame the eyes.

APPLICATION PROCEDURE: A small angle brush should be used for applying pressed powder shadow. For detailed application use an eye-liner brush when the powder is moistened.

The first step is to analyze your brow shape. (Refer to "Creating a Balanced Brow", for guidelines.) If your brows are correctly shaped and require no colour correction, all you need to do is brush the brows in shape using a small brow brush. Although brow makeup can make a world of difference in correcting the brows, it is not always necessary. Apply the brow colour in short feathery strokes following the direction of the hair growth. *Never* draw in brows with straight lines. When brow makeup is completed, brush them to achieve a softer, more natural-looking effect.

Scene VIII

Eye shading

Shading the brow bone is the first step in shadow structuring the eyes. By adding depth to this naturally receded area which is from the beginning of the orbital bone (crease line), into its sloped section, the eyes will in contrast, be enhanced and appear larger and more prominent.

Remember the principle of contouring: Dark and flat muted colours recede and minimize, light or bright ones bring an area forward.

By shading you can also recede prominence, reduce puffiness or lift drooping eyelids.

Shadows are available in a variety of forms — creams, powders, and soft pencils in flat or pearlized. Highly frosted shadows are not suitable for shading, even if the tone is dark. The high frost content has an adverse effect and brings emphasis to the area instead of setting it back.

APPLICATION PROCEDURE: A rounded fluff brush is a must when using a powder shadow in order to achieve a natural and easy application. For cream, use a medium straight shadow brush. The basic shading is applied to the natural slope of the brow bone, from the inner to the outer corner. Keep the shadow inside the guideline used for brow placement.

Pick up small amounts of shadow each time, then dab on your hand to remove the excess. Start the application at the crease, moving the brush up in light feathery strokes. With this method the natural inward slope of the brow bone picks up the shading colour in the correct area. Do not move the brush over the upper ledge of the brow bone. The inner and outer corner should be blended carefully to avoid telltale lines of separation. (Refer to "Corrective eye contouring" for special instructions.)

Scene IX

Lid shadow

Lid shadow is used to brighten, enhance and intensify the eyes. When eye shadow is not used the eyes can appear dull and faded.

Choose a medium tone shade to complement your eye colouring or clothing. The colour choice is important, however, in many cases it is the incorrect application of the colour depth or placement that is one of the common mistakes women make in applying eye makeup. Keep in mind that you don't want to detract from the eyes — you want to enhance them. The type of product used for eyelid application is a matter of personal choice; cream, powder, or soft pencils in flat or pearlized are all suitable.

APPLICATION PROCEDURE: Using a flat eye shadow brush, apply the shadow from the roots of the upper lashes to the crease of the lid. Blend lightly up into the shading. Keep the lid colour inside the guideline used for brow placement, blending off into invisibility. (For exceptions refer to "Corrective eye contouring".)

Scene X

Eye highlight

The third step in shadow structuring the eyes is to highlight the brow bone. Cream, pressed powder or liquid cream shadow, soft pencils or iridescent dusts can be used. Choose a tone that is lighter than the shading and lid colours. Avoid the use of white as it is too garish and unnatural.

APPLICATION PROCEDURE: Apply the colour with a straight shadow brush, starting about one quarter of the way in from the beginning of the brow, blending out to the end and down to the shading. Blend off to invisibility at the inner corner of the brow.

The highlighting must be very light and subtle. If the application is too heavy or the colour is too stark the purpose of this step is lost. Remember, this step should appear as a natural emphasis of reflection of light, not an obvious band of colour.

Correct blending is crucial to the overall effect of the three shadow colours used. You should never be able to see where one actually begins and the other ends. The objective is to create a smooth flow of colours and tones. If further blending is required, use a clean fluff brush and lightly brush over the entire area to soften and perfect the blending.

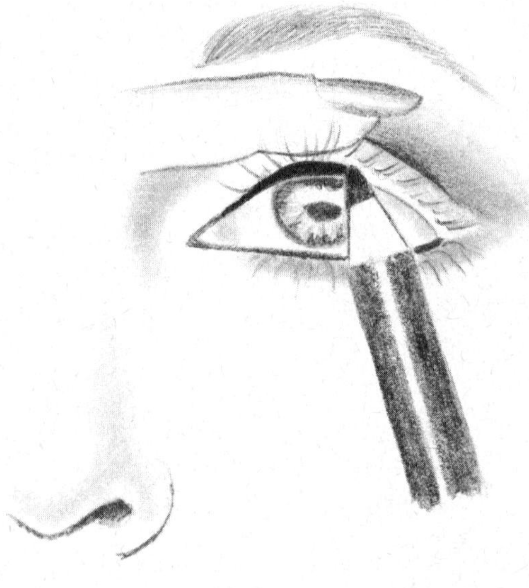

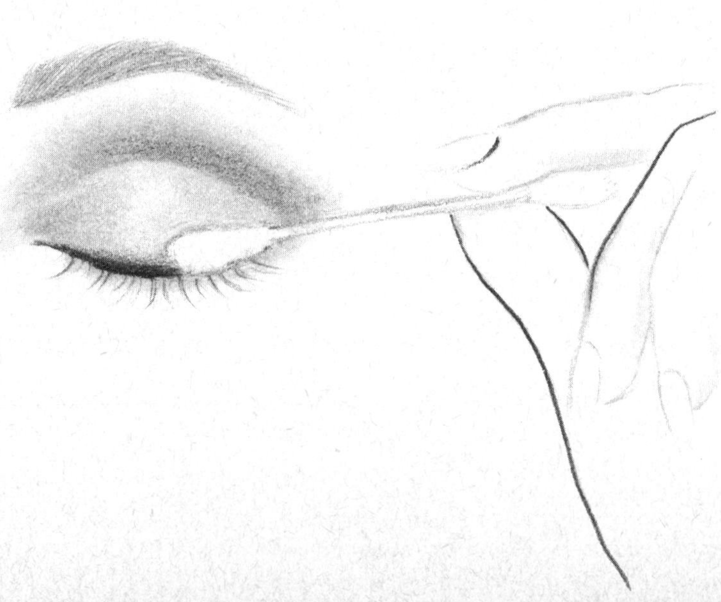

Scene XI

Eyeliner

The main purpose of using an eyeliner is to make the lashes appear thicker and the eyes larger. Understanding the reason for this step will help to avoid making mistakes with this application.

First of all, your colour selection is very important. Choose a colour that is equal to, or darker than the colour used for shading, or one that complements the other shadows used on the eyes. Light and bright bold colour surrounding the eye is unnatural, unflattering and totally defeats the purpose of eyelining. The idea is to enlarge the eye by defining and creating the illusion of thicker lashes, not detract from them by drawing attention to an obvious band of colour.

The products most successfully used for eyelining include pressed powder shadow, (dry or moist) and soft pencils in shades such as smoky grey, deep plum, brown, charcoal, black, and colours that are deep muted or smoky in tone.

APPLICATION PROCEDURE: When using pressed powder shadow use a fine-tipped eyeliner brush. Start the application at the inner corner where the natural lashes start to grow. Apply among, and just above the lashes in short strokes, not one single line. This technique achieves a softer application and also avoids pulling on the fragile eye tissue. Continue with the same procedure under and into the bottom lashes starting slightly out from the inner corner. For a wide-eyed effect start the outline at about the centre of the eye. With a double end applicator, or small angled brush, lightly blend and smudge the edges until the application is imperceptible as a definite line. The result produced should be a soft smudged smoky look, so subtle it is not really noticed, but the effect is there.

A soft pencil can also be applied along the inner, upper and lower rims to further dramatize the eyes. Holding the eye area taut with the fingers, move the pencil softly back and forth inside the eye rims to achieve the desired intensity. Your colour choice for applying the pencil to the inner rims does not have to be the same as used for the outlining, although the shade should harmonize with the other eye colours used.

You can make green eyes appear darker by applying a light shade of green, or make them look paler by using a deep smoky toned green.

Make blue eyes look darker, and the whites of the eyes whiter with a light or medium blue. They will take on a lighter appearance by using a dark blue or navy blue.

Violet will give blue eyes a violet hue, in addition to making dark eyes appear darker.

Augment the fullness of the lash line by lining the upper rim with a coal or charcoal colour.

For dramatic smoky depth to the eyes, apply one of the darker soft pencils to both the upper and lower rims.

Scene XII

Mascara

If you could choose only one makeup item for the eyes, mascara would be the best choice, as no other single product dramatizes the eyes more.

Mascara is used to create darker, thicker, and longer lashes and is available in waterproof and thickening formulas. Black, charcoal or dark brown are suitable for the majority of women, soft brown is recommended especially for very fair colouring to achieve natural eye emphasis.

APPLICATION PROCEDURE: For those not blessed with curly lashes, an eyelash curler is a very important beauty aid. Curled lashes enhance and give the eye a larger, more open look. Eyelash curlers should be used prior to mascara application. Place the curler at the base of the lashes, and squeeze firmly for a few seconds, several times. This method is more effective than squeezing firmly in one place for a longer period, as this tends to give a bent look to the lashes.

Apply mascara to both the upper and lower lashes, working from the base (root) to the tip, making sure each and every hair is embedded into the brush. Now brush the lashes with a small brow brush to ensure that they are separated. Dab a little loose powder or powder shadow on your finger and dust onto the lashes. Reapply the mascara. Brush again if necessary. This technique will make your lashes appear longer and more lush.

Scene XIII

Lip colour

Moist, luscious lips are the finishing touch to your makeup. The reason for using a lip colour is to brighten the face, as well as balance the makeup, and protect the lips to keep them soft and supple.

The first step in applying lip colour is to use a lip pencil. Lip outlining perfects, corrects, and emphasizes the shape of the lips, and also prevents lipstick from "bleeding" into tiny lines that form around the mouth.

Select a lipstick to harmonize with the other makeup used. Regular or pearlized lipsticks are available in rich creamy moisturizing formulas. (Refer to "Colour plan" for guidelines.)

Finish off with a lip gloss, to intensify the lush shiny look of your lip colour and to provide added protection against dryness. Lip gloss can also be used alone to achieve a moist shiny effect when a subtle tone is desired. Colour choice depends on the effect you wish to achieve. Shades can be matched to the lipstick colour, or chosen to complement colour tone variation.

NOTE: Try mixing one of the "iridescent dusts" into your lipstick for a unique ultra-pearlized effect.

APPLICATION PROCEDURE: To outline the lips, apply lip pencil from the centre bow to the corners, gently following the natural contour of the mouth using a series of short strokes. On the lower lip, follow the natural curves from the centre to the corners, or if you feel more comfortable, reverse the application, starting from the corners to the centre. (Refer to "Correcting the lips" for special instruction.)

For best results, always use a lip brush when applying lipstick. Blend the colour into the lip outline to avoid presenting two distinctly different shades between the lip liner and the lipstick colour.

Apply the lip sheen also using the lip brush. Concentrate the sheen more in the middle of the lips, rather than up to the lip line.

It is important to your total look to check and reapply your lip colour when it is necessary during the day. With continual talking, licking the lips and eating and drinking, it is impossible for your lip colour to stay intact all day. Lips have a tendency to get parched and dry-looking which can be most unflattering. In addition, the absence of colour can give a dull, washed-out appearance to the face. Keep in mind that even though the eyes may be the focal point, attention is constantly drawn to the lips as you speak and smile. Make them the kind of lips that are worth looking at.

Scene XIV

Evaluation

Now is the time to step back and look into a good sized, well lighted makeup mirror at the total effect. A must for day makeup. If you are going to be outdoors double check your makeup carefully, examining your face in the natural light.

Ask yourself if any one area is too obvious. Are the eyes too definite in relation to the lips? Remember the section on "Colour plan"? You should create a sense of balance with the depth of colours used. For example soft eyes, soft lips, etc.

Is the facial shading noticeable, or, is there no effect from the shading at all?

Has the cheek colour faded, or, is it too bright and unnatural?

Do the eye shading, lid colour, or highlighter stand out too prominently, or, do noticeable lines of demarcation show?

Does the eye outline look too sharp and definite?

What about foundation and powder? Is the coverage natural? Is it blended correctly? Are there any demarcation lines showing?

Is the total effect appropriate for the occasion?

Once you answer all these questions you may have to add to some area, or tone down others, or pick up appropriate brushes and blend again to perfect the application. In the makeup steps, this "Scene" is as important as all the others in learning to become your own makeup artist. Make it a habit, and you will be surprised at how critical you become in re-examining your application, and how much you will learn by taking the extra time and being aware of what to look for.

SHADOW VARIATIONS

The basic rules for eye shadow application as covered in our basic principle chapter suggest a medium tone on the eye lid; a dark hue in the crease to add depth to the eyes; a paler shade under the brow for highlighting. However, many exciting effects may be produced by variation in eye shadow placement.

Your particular eye shape should be considered as to the suitability of some of these variations — they are not for everyone. Experiment to find the effect that is most flattering for you.

To the basic shadow application, add a deeper tone just above the crease to create definite depth to the eyes, a look still associated with those famous Garbo eyes.

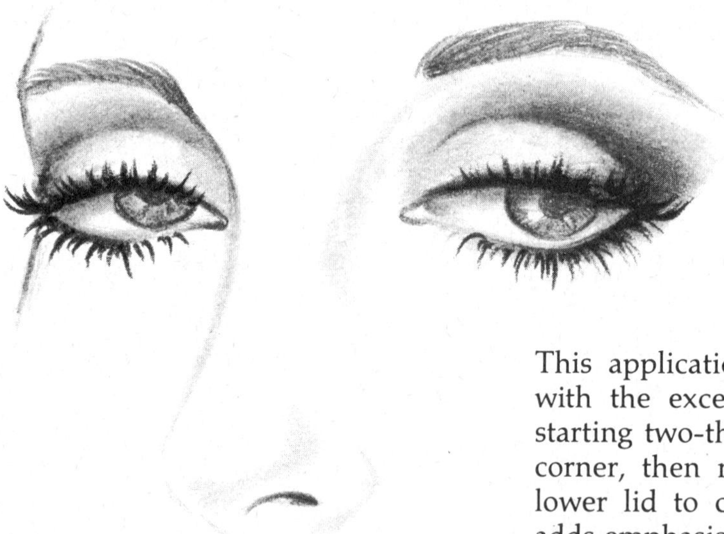

This application is similar to the above with the exception of the added depth starting two-thirds over toward the outer corner, then moving in on the top and lower lid to create a triangle. This step adds emphasis to the outer corner, as well as being an excellent step in "lifting" drooping eyes.

Apply basic steps for shading and highlight. For the lid, apply a lighter tone to the inner half and a deeper tone to the outer half. You could use light to medium shadow or medium to dark, depending on the effect you wish to achieve.

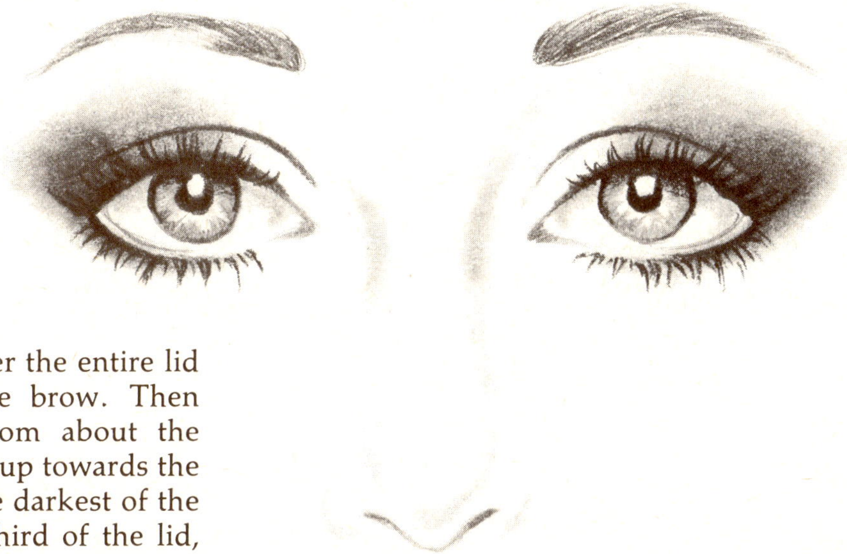

Apply the lightest tone over the entire lid from the lashes up to the brow. Then apply a medium tone from about the centre of the eye in a slant up towards the brow. The third colour, the darkest of the three, starts at the outer third of the lid, moving up and out slightly beyond the end of the brow, and down under the outer corner of the under eye. This is more of a fun fashion look, definitely not for everyone. The eye should have balanced proportion to be able to carry this look off effectively.

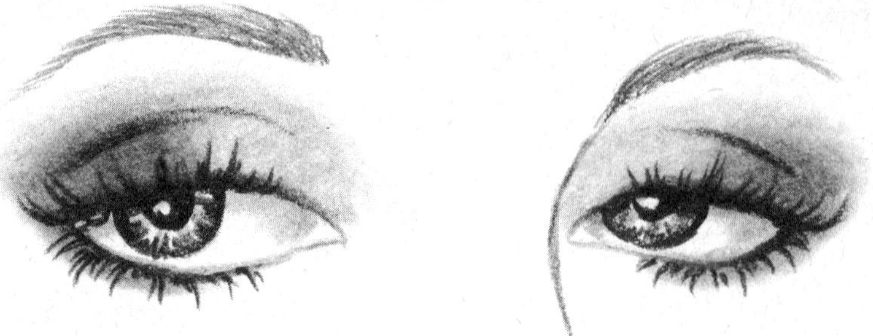

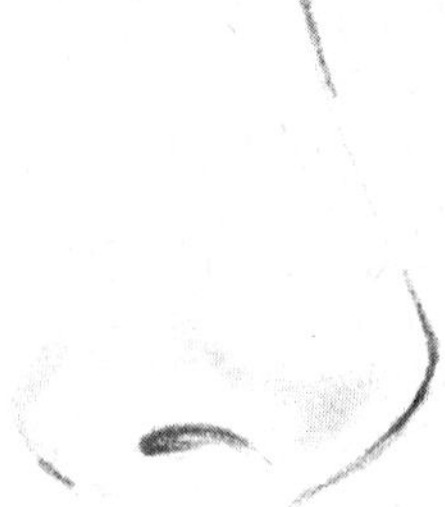

Apply a medium-toned shadow to the inner half of the eye from the lashes up into the slope of the brow bone. Start the deeper shade beginning half way across the lid, blending up into the brow bone, and out slightly beyond the outer corner. Highlight just below the brow. This shadow application is popular for achieving a wide-eyed look, and is also effective for close-set eyes.

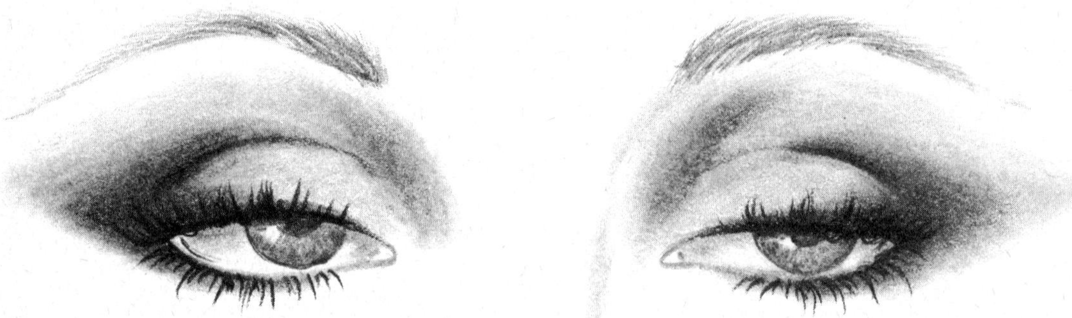

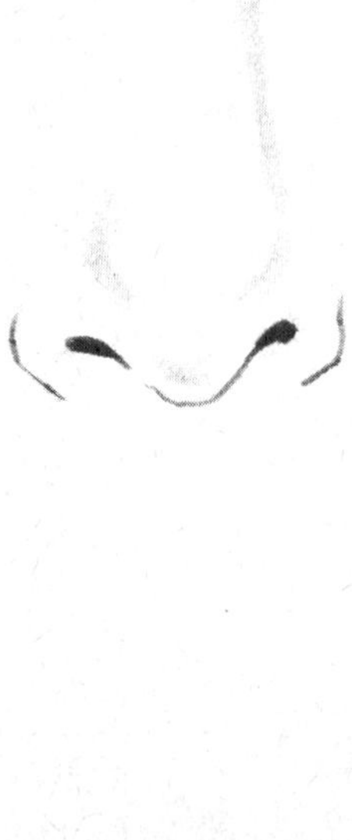

From the lashes to just under the brow apply a base of medium-toned shadow. Brush a deeper tone from the inner corner, slanting up towards the beginning of the brow. Using the same colour, continue the application starting at the crease about half way across the eye, blending out beyond the corner and under the bottom lashes, forming a side-shaped V (>) to give an almond or slanted effect.

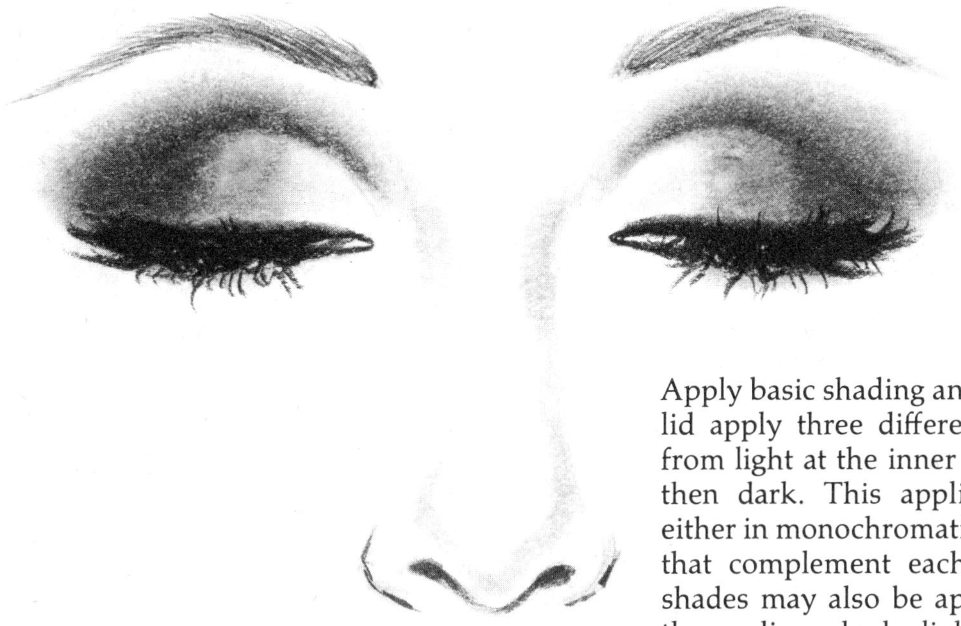

Apply basic shading and highlight. For the lid apply three different shades, moving from light at the inner corner to medium, then dark. This application is effective either in monochromatic shades or colours that complement each other. The three shades may also be applied starting with the medium shade, light in the centre and the deeper shade on the outer corner.

To the basic lid shadow application add a lighter tone of shadow, or highlighting stardust to the centre of the lid. This gives the effect of opening up the eye, and is also very effective in widening narrow, almond eyes.

NOTES